D1072044

Mardi Gras, Gumbo, and Zydeco

Mardi Gras, Gumbo, and Zydeco

Readings in Louisiana Culture

EDITED BY MARCIA GAUDET
JAMES C. MCDONALD

University Press of Mississippi
Jackson

www.upress.state.ms.us

Copyright © 2003 by University Press of Mississippi
All rights reserved
Manufactured in the United States of America

11 10 09 08 07 06 05 04 03 4 3 2 1
∞

Library of Congress Cataloging-in-Publication Data

Mardi Gras, gumbo, and zydeco : readings in Louisiana culture /
edited by Marcia Gaudet, James C. McDonald.
   p. cm.
Includes bibliographical references and index.
  ISBN 1-57806-529-1 (alk. paper) – ISBN 1-57806-530-5
  (pbk. : alk. paper)
  1. Louisiana–Civilization. 2. Louisiana–Social life and customs.
3. Popular culture–Louisiana. 4. Folklore–Louisiana. I. Gaudet,
Marcia G. II. McDonald, James C.
  F369.5 .M37 2003
  306'.09763–dc21   2002009708

British Library Cataloging-in-Publication Data available

Frontis: Cypress Swamp, University of Louisiana at Lafayette,
1994. Photo by Marcia Gaudet.

Contents

Mardi Gras, Gumbo, and Zydeco

An Introduction to Louisiana Culture

MARCIA GAUDET

Louisiana has been described in many ways—"south of the South," "the northern tip of the Caribbean," "this folklore land." South Louisiana's culture is different not only from the rest of the United States, but also from the rest of the South and even from the northern half of Louisiana itself. A professor who recently moved back to Kentucky after retiring from University of Louisiana at Lafayette wrote to a friend that he was moving back "to the states." Whether it's the French and Spanish influence, the unique mixture of Cajun and Creole, the blending of African, Caribbean, and Native American influences, or a combination of all of these, Louisiana merits the description given by Pulitzer Prize winning author Robert Penn Warren: "After Louisiana, nothing else is real."

Louisiana is a state with at least two distinctively different cultural regions—predominantly French Catholic southern Louisiana and predominantly Anglo Prostestant northern Louisiana. Mardi Gras, gumbo, and zydeco—three of the topics covered in this book—are all part of the culture of southern Louisiana (including New Orleans). They are vital examples of southern Louisiana folklife, the living traditions of the culture. The readings in this book reflect the culture, folklore, and folklife of southern Louisiana and some of its important ethnic and religious groups. It is important to note, however, that Cajuns and Creoles are also a part of American culture, and they share many cultural traditions, narratives, holidays, foodways, and styles of music with the rest of the country.

The essays in *Mardi Gras, Gumbo, and Zydeco* provide both an introduction to aspects of Louisiana's culture that may not be generally known as well as insights into cultural traditions of diverse ethnic groups in Louisiana. These include Louisiana celebrations of Mardi Gras and Christmas, Louisiana food-ways, Cajun and Creole beliefs, Native Americans in Louisiana, Zydeco music, and Cajun humor. Understanding the important things in a culture—including its language, music, foodways, traditions, and celebrations—is essential to understanding the people.

The culture's complexity is enriched by the long interac-tion of French, Africans (particularly Senegambian), Spanish, Germans, Creoles, Cajuns, and Native Americans with each other, as well as with later immigrant groups, such as Haitians, Irish, Italians, Croatians, Isleños (descendents of Canary Islanders), and Vietnamese. In addition to the Houmas, other important Native American groups still vital in Louisiana are the Chitimacha (in Charenton), the Koasati (in Elton), and the Tunica-Biloxi (in Marksville).

Cajuns and Creoles

Cajuns and Creoles, while maintaining strong cultural and ethnic identities, are also part of mainstream American and Southern culture. The terms Cajun and Creole are often con-fused and misunderstood. Even within Louisiana culture, there is not universal agreement on the meaning and use of these terms, particularly Creole. There are, however, generally agreed upon historical definitions of these terms.

Louisiana Cajuns are a diverse group (including the Prairie Cajuns, the Wetland Cajuns, and the River Cajuns) who share common bonds of traditions and language. They are descen-dants of the Acadians, colonists from France who first settled Acadie (now Nova Scotia) in the maritime region of Canada in 1604, one of the earliest settlements in North America. By the 1670s, the Acadians in Canada had become a distinctive frontier culture—basically peasant, rural, French, Catholic, family-oriented, ruggedly individualistic, with a fierce sense of personal dignity. In 1720, the British obtained permanent possession of the colony from France and re-named it

Nova Scotia ("New Scotland" or *Nouvelle Écosse* to the French-speaking Acadians). After much turmoil and the refusal of the Acadians to swear an oath of allegiance to the British, in 1755 the British seized the property of the Acadians and forced them into exile, the diaspora known as *le Grand Derangement*. The largest group of the over 6000 exiled Acadians eventually made their way to semi-tropical Louisiana. Louisiana had been a French possession since 1682 and already had a large, established French population. Ironically, by the time the Acadians began to arrive, Louisiana had been ceded to Spain (1762), and remained a Spanish possession until 1800 when it was ceded back to France. France did not take formal possession of Louisiana until 1803, and in the same year it was sold by Napoleon to the United States.

The Acadians who came to Louisiana in the 1760s had, for the most part, been away from France for well over a century, and they had little in common with the French Creoles in New Orleans, who tended to feel superior because of their education, culture, and wealth, and because they spoke a more standard French than the Acadians. The Acadians (who became 'Cadiens, and then Cajuns) settled in the areas along the Mississippi River north of New Orleans (the River Cajuns); the areas along Bayou Lafourche, Bayou Terrebonne, Bayou Teche, and the Atchafalaya Swamp (the Wetland Cajuns); and on the prairies of southwest Louisiana (the Prairie Cajuns). The area of Cajun settlement in southern Louisiana forms a triangle with the base running along the Gulf Coast of Louisiana west of New Orleans and the apex in central Louisiana. All Cajuns shared a heritage and traditions from shared experiences, but each group also adapted to a lifestyle based on the environment. Because of their isolation (both self-imposed and geographic) and their shared language, the Cajuns developed a distinctive culture in southern Louisiana that combines a heritage from France, from the Canadian maritime experience, and from Louisiana. They also incorporated traditions, folkways, and music from those closest to them—Native Americans, Spanish, French, German, and African American. For further discussion of the Cajuns, see especially Carl Brasseaux's works on the history of the Cajuns and Barry Jean Ancelet's works on Cajun folklore.

The term *Creole* is harder to define precisely, and Creole identity tends to be more confusing and more complex. *Creole* was originally used in Louisiana to designate people of European or African heritage born in the colonies (as opposed to those who immigrated to the colonies). In the nineteenth century, particularly in New Orleans, Creole came to be used to designate specifically white Creoles and the term *Creoles of Color* was used to designate those of African or mixed heritage. These usages are reflected in the writings of nineteenth century authors such as Kate Chopin and George Washington Cable. During the twentieth century, usage of the term *Creole* changed dramatically. At present, the term *Creole* is used in Louisiana to designate anything that is "home-grown" or native to Louisiana—*e.g.*, Creole tomatoes. When applied to people, it is commonly used to designate people of mixed African and French heritage and culture, particularly those who are light-skinned and who are part of the southern Louisiana French Catholic culture. This usage is clearly reflected by contemporary Louisiana writers such as Ernest J. Gaines. In vernacular usage today, the term *Creole* seems to be more inclusive, denoting anyone who is a part of Afro-French American heritage, culture, or community in Louisiana.

Creole is an elusive term that seems to shift in meaning both in time and place. The only thing generally agreed upon is that the term excludes Cajuns. Works by Virginia Dominguez, Gwendolyn Midlo Hall, James Dormon, and others have illustrated the ever changing usages of the term Creole. Dominguez suggests being born and raised in the French-dominated Louisiana society was more significant than race as a determination of who was Creole in the period prior to Americanization (Dominguez 1986). From the mid-nineteenth century, the term Creole of Color was used as a term of somewhat exclusive ethnic identity and pride by a self-aware group of people who were Afro-European, Catholic, historically French speaking, and often property owners (Dormon 1995: 166–67). Sometime during the twentieth century, this special ethnic identity was more commonly called simply Creole, and it tended to be racially defined. Dominguez says that in New Orleans in the 1970s, there was a distinction between Creole and Black. More recently, as Dormon points out, "the term 'black Creole' has come into more common, and less precise usage," clearly implying a more inclusive usage and possibly including "the entire African-American ('black') population of south Louisiana" (Dormon 1996: 166). Hall says: "*Creole* has come to mean the language and the folk culture that was native to the southern part of Louisiana where African, French, and Spanish influence was most deeply rooted historically and culturally" (Hall 1992: 157).

Readings—South Louisiana's Culture, People, and Living Traditions

Mardi Gras has been celebrated in southern Louisiana since the French first settled in the area. Mardi Gras (or Fat Tuesday) marks the day before Ash Wednesday, the beginning of Lent, and a time of repentance in the Catholic Church. The first four chapters present different Mardi Gras performances and customs in Louisiana.

Chapter 1, "Mardi Gras and the Media: Who's Fooling Whom?" by Barry Jean Ancelet, is a description of the Cajun Country Mardi Gras on the prairies of southwestern Louisiana and an examination of the media coverage, which has often misrepresented this ritual. This *courir de Mardi Gras* involves begging rituals with masked horseback riders in the quest to obtain chickens, rice, etc., for a community gumbo. Though the rural *courir de Mardi Gras* was suspended in Mamou and other places, to be revived later, many of the country Mardi Gras rides or "runs," particularly those in isolated areas of the southwestern Louisiana prairie, have been continuous. These are the ones most likely to have retained the most "primitive" elements, such as ritual whippings.

Chapter 2, "Buffalo Bill and the Mardi Gras Indians" by Michael P. Smith, traces a possible origin for the African American tradition of street parading in New Orleans. This cultural enactment involves Native American costuming, particularly the ornate feathered headdresses of the Plains

Indians. Michael Smith's article presents an interesting, though controversial, explanation for a possible origin of the New Orleans Mardi Gras Indians. Not all scholars agree with Smith's focus or conclusions, but it seems likely that the Buffalo Bill show was one influence on the style of Mardi Gras Indian costuming. Important African and Caribbean influences are evident as well, and they have been well documented by others, such as Kalamu ya Salaam. John Nunley and Judith Bettelheim note the influence of Caribbean festival arts on the Mardi Gras Indians. Robert Thompson's studies of Yoruba performance style in ritual and play suggest important African influences (Nunley and Bettelheim 1988; see also Kalamu ya Salaam 1997).

Chapter 3, "Every Man a King: Worldview, Social Tension, and Carnival in New Orleans" by Frank de Caro and Tom Ireland, is an examination of the social implications of New Orleans Mardi Gras parades involving carnival krewes, floats, and crowds "begging" for carnival throws, beads, and doubloons, the most well-known Mardi Gras performance format. As de Caro and Ireland point out, "Public celebrations and public performances are enacted because they have 'meanings' for those who enact them. They communicate ideas, beliefs, and feelings and may often constitute complex symbol systems designed to interconnect attitudes and emotions." They suggest that one function of New Orleans Mardi Gras is to serve as a symbolic unifier of diverse groups and attitudes, at least for that day. Their statement that the carnival krewes are "all white organizations" is now outdated. Following a New Orleans City Council ordinance in December 1991, all krewes that seek a permit to parade on city streets cannot restrict membership on the basis of race, religion, etc. At that time, Comus, Momus and Proteus chose not to parade, but remained private clubs. Others, such of the Krewe of Rex, opened their membership, most notably to African Americans. One might also take issue with de Caro and Ireland's statements about flambeau carriers. Flambeau carriers are now usually regarded as a select group who are generally admired as skilled performers (not as a subservient class, as the article suggests at that time).

Chapter 4, "Mardi Gras Chase" by Glen Pitre, is an examination of a remnant of earlier Mardi Gras traditions that involve mock chasing and "whipping" of young boys. This is one of the oldest Mardi Gras traditions in Louisiana and certainly one liable to provoke misunderstanding and criticism from outsiders. Pitre presents the perspective of the insiders in explaining why this tradition continues in isolated areas in southern Louisiana.

Chapter 5, "The New Orleans King Cake in Southwest Louisiana" by Marcia Gaudet, traces the tradition of the Twelfth Night or Epiphany cake from Europe to New Orleans to southwestern Louisiana and examines the contemporary aspects of this popular custom. The King Cake tradition continues to be extremely popular throughout southern Louisiana and hundreds of thousands of King Cakes are shipped out of Louisiana each year.

Chapter 6, "Christmas Bonfires in South Louisiana: Tradition and Innovation" by Marcia Gaudet, describes the contemporary tradition of lighting bonfires on the levees of the Mississippi River between New Orleans and Baton Rouge, and gives some probable sources and routes of transmission. The bonfires continue to be popular in the river parishes area. One religious innovation in recent years is the St. Vincent de Paul Society bonfire, a bonfire with a traditional teepee-shaped pyre with an opening in front to form a nativity creche. Life size statues of the holy family are placed in the creche/bonfire and removed before the fire is lit on Christmas eve. In 1993, there was a spectacular replica of the Louisiana State Capitol. It included wooden stairs, with the name of a different state on each, leading up to the Capitol, in imitation of the State Capitol in Baton Rouge (which is typically not called the "State House" in Louisiana).

Chapter 7, "The Creole Tradition" by Michael Tisserand, is an article about traditional Afro-French music in Louisiana, focusing on the "heroes" of Louisiana French Creole music, known as "la la," which later developed into what is now called zydeco. The great Creole musicians include Amede Ardoin, Canray Fontenot, and Bois-Sec Ardoin. Since this essay was first published in 1994, Creole music-influenced zydeco has continued to be increasingly popular throughout the United States and beyond. In 2001, an article about zydeco appeared on the front page of the *Wall Street Journal.* Canray Fontenot, who is featured in this piece, always said that he did not play "zydeco." Until his death in 1995, however, he did play the distinctive Creole music that gave zydeco its roots. Popular zydeco musicians today include Geno Delafose, C.J. Chenier (son of zydeco great Clifton Chenier), Nathan Williams and the Zydeco ChaCha's, Terrance Simien, and Buckwheat Zydeco.

Chapter 8, "Hidden Nation: The Houmas Speak" by Barbara Sillery, is an article on both the historical routes and the contemporary identity of the Houma Indians of Golden Meadow, Dulac, and other coastal towns in southern Louisiana. Historically a peaceful tribe, they had no treaties with the U.S. to prove their existence. By the early 19th century, the Houmas were considered a "vanished" tribe by the Bureau of Indian Affairs. The Houmas obtained official recognition by the State of Louisiana in 1977, but they have still not obtained tribal recognition by the Federal Government.

Chapter 9, "Some Accounts of Witch Riding" by Patricia K. Rickels, was first published in the early 1960s. It gives first person accounts of *cauchemar* or nocturnal assault experiences in Louisiana. Though some of the language reflects word usage that is now dated, the article gives valuable insights into beliefs that are still known among African Americans and Cajuns in rural areas and small towns in southwestern Louisiana. This is reflected in contemporary recordings such as "Kushmal" by Zydeco Force and creative writing such as Darrell Bourque's poem "Cauchemar."

Chapter 10, "Charlene Richard: Folk Veneration among the Cajuns" by Marcia Gaudet, examines the local or regional devotion to a young Catholic girl whom many believe to be a saint. Since shortly after her death in 1959, visitors (including busloads of tourists) have come to her grave in Richard, Louisiana. It has become an important pilgrimage site, and the anniversary of her death is observed each year with a memorial Mass. The highway on which the church and cemetery are located has recently been renamed "Charlene

Richard Highway." In 2001, a group of Cajun musicians, Ray Richard and Family and Friends (including one of Charlene's brothers and several of her cousins) recorded a CD entitled "The Cajun Saint." The CD cover has a picture of Charlene, and the lyrics of the title song present the story of Charlene's death and the legend of this local saint.

Chapter 11, "Ôte Voir Ta Sacrée Soutane: Anti-Clerical Humor in French Louisiana" by Barry Jean Ancelet, is an examination of Cajun humor involving priests and their roles in Cajun and Creole culture. The Catholic Church is a powerful institution in southern Louisiana, and the great majority of Cajuns and Creoles are Roman Catholics. Oral tradition also shows irreverence and anti-clerical humor.

Chapter 12, "The Social and Symbolic Uses of Ethnic/ Regional Foodways: Cajuns and Crawfish in South Louisiana" by C. Paige Gutierrez, discusses the crawfish as a symbol of ethnic and regional identity in south Louisiana. Images of the crawfish as symbol seem to appear almost everywhere, including t-shirts, books, souvenirs, napkins, advertisements, and signs. The crawfish boil has become a cultural ritual that may serve to strengthen Cajun community ties.

Chapter 13, "Is It Cajun, or Is It Creole?" by Marcia Gaudet, is a brief discussion of the similarities and differences in Cajun and Creole cooking and food customs. Louisiana foodways have earned the acclaim of travelers and writers, and New Orleans cuisine has long enjoyed a reputation for excellence. Mark Twain said in *Life on the Mississippi* that a pompano dinner in a New Orleans restaurant was "delicious as the less criminal forms of sin." In the last two decades, Louisiana's Cajun and Creole foods, in general, have been lauded as regional foodways of international distinction.

All of the readings in this book have been previously published. Since the original publications are no longer readily accessible, this book will hopefully make them available to a wide audience of readers interested in culture, folklife, and traditions of southern Louisiana.

Works Cited
All works cited are listed in "Suggestions for Further Reading."

Mardi Gras, Gumbo, and Zydeco

Mardi Gras and the Media
Who's Fooling Whom?

BARRY JEAN ANCELET

Journalists routinely travel far and wide to report on what's happening in the country and the world. Their human interest pieces are all the information most of the public has on other people and their culture. Yet reporters often lack the kind of ethnological background to understand the cultures they encounter. Consequently, they frequently produce interpretations considered inaccurate by concerned folklorists and community members, interpretations which misinform their viewers, listeners and readers. This chapter examines popular media coverage of the south Louisiana prairie Mardi Gras celebration and some of its unusual (and erroneous) interpretations as a case study of intercultural misunderstanding.

Though issued from the same liturgical tradition as its counterparts in New Orleans, Rio de Janeiro, and Nice, the Cajun Mardi Gras differs substantially from them. Rooted in the medieval European *fête de la quémande*, the *course du Mardi Gras* is related to other ceremonial begging traditions like Christmas caroling and trick-or-treating in which a procession of revelers travels through the countryside bringing their performance with them to various homes and requesting a gift in exchange (Ancelet 1980; Lindahl 1984; Spitzer 1987; Ancelet 1987). The Mardi Gras riders seek ingredients for a communal gumbo served at the end of the day. The most interesting gift is a live chicken which the riders catch themselves despite their costumes and varying states of inebriation.

From *Southern Folklore* 46:3 (1989): 211–19. Reprinted by permission of University Press of Kentucky.

Mardi Gras dancing to the music from the music wagon,
Church Point, 2001. Photo by Marcia Gaudet.

They sing and dance, display their masks and costumes, and
play roles ranging from the clown to the outlaw, all activities
fueled by the ritualized consumption of alcohol. At the end of
the day they return to town to eat the fruits of their labor and
to dance in a masked ball which ends the festive period
and ushers in Lent, traditionally a season of fasting and
sacrifice.

Some celebrations retain surprising primitive and medieval
survivals. In Kinder and Iota, for example, participants pre-
tend to whip each other with rolled burlap sacks while walking through the countryside. In earlier years, because
concealing identities behind masks conferred impunity on the
riders, Mardi Gras often became a day of reckoning, so often
that in the 1940s the celebration was suspended. It was revived
in Mamou in the 1950s with strict rules which gave absolute
authority to a capitaine and his assistants in order to contain
the ritual chaos. The controls established by Paul Tate and
Revon Reed in Mamou have served as a model for numerous
communities throughout south Louisiana which have
revived their own versions of the Mardi Gras. In Mamou and
Church Point, the oldest and largest of the revivals, there may
be as many as 200 to 300 masked and costumed horsemen
who charge farmhouses at full gallop when the Capitaine

waves a white flag to signal that a family has agreed to receive their visit.

For the outsider the Cajun Mardi Gras is exotic, colorful and picturesque. Because of its obvious "quaintness," the Cajun Mardi Gras attracts many journalists and documentary film-makers looking for local color stories (*e.g.*, Blank 1972; Blank 1973; Brunot 1974; Goldsmith 1975; McCallum 1980; Audet 1982; Spitzer and Duplantier 1984). Unfortunately many who visit the Mardi Gras are simply fascinated with the strange-ness of it all. They often do not seek out background infor-mation to help understand and subsequently explain the underlying complexities. Even if they do, they usually are so blinded by the surface glare that they forget whatever they learned by the time they get back to their word processors or editing rooms. Consequently they usually portray the Mardi Gras only as a surreal procession of masked drunks falling all over themselves, chasing chickens, and sometimes maiming the chickens and themselves in the process.

Media coverage of cultural events is already difficult because of time limits and deadlines (Fisherman 1980: 34–37). Reporters invariably need to describe the historical and cul-tural background of an event in a line or two. Journalists readily agree that the combination of deadlines and target audience levels don't allow for the preservation of nuances and complexities, especially in the area called "soft news" (71–72). Reporters often cut off interviews with statements like "That's enough, really. Nobody's going to understand all the details" and "We can only cover the broad strokes." An NBC camera operator working on a story on two 1986 National Heritage Award recipients paraphrased the standard line from network headquarters: "Not too much of that stuff. We don't want to put the audience off. We just need enough offbeat to syncopate the real news. A little bit of that goes a long way, you know." It is difficult to avoid stereotypes and oversim-plification in any folklife coverage, and Mardi Gras, which is designed to invert reality and mock the observer, only com-pounds the problem.

In 1978, when the New Orleans Mardi Gras was threat-ened by a police strike, ABC sent a 20/20 crew to cover the story and the producer discovered an interesting twist in the fact that the prairie Cajun Mardi Gras was unaffected by the New Orleans strike. This eventually developed into a story which was given the catchy title, "The Mardi Gras They Couldn't Stop" (Brim 1978). The producer met with local sources during her initial research trip to get some background on the celebration. She also described the "story" as they saw it from New York. I met with her at length to explain the cultural and historical significance of the Mardi Gras and the place of the Cajun *course du Mardi Gras* in the larger scheme of things. After several days, I was confident that I had succeeded in getting her to reconsider this cultural event on its own terms without hauling in preconceived notions from New York. But by the time the correspondent and crew flew in later, the producer had tossed aside most of what she had learned and at once became the leader of a journalistic safari into Cajun country.

On Sunday the crew went to Church Point to film that town's version of the Mardi Gras and predictably incurred the wrath and ridicule of the riders by getting in the way of the procession and asking obvious questions. At one point, having arrived late at the house with the longest driveway and consequently the most dramatic charge, they even requested that the Capitaine redo the charge, not only disrupting the natural course of the day but also breaking a rule of broadcast journalism not to stage events. At the same time the crew apparently found it difficult to throttle back on their usual hard news approach and misapplied investigative journalism on an unsuspecting cultural event. Much of the piece centered on the heavy use of alcohol during this rite of passage. Instead of telling the cultural story of the Mardi Gras, the piece became a sort of Mardi Gras-gate story which focused primarily on the bizarre distortion of reality created by the juxtaposition of masks and alcohol with real people and examined the country Mardi Gras as a durable (read obstinate) counterpart to the New Orleans party in jeopardy.

Even the most respected journalists are not immune from coming in with a ready-made story. In 1977 two separate NPR crews came to the Mamou area to cover the Mardi Gras. One worked with folklorist Nick Spitzer to cover the black Creole run around Duralde for *Folk Festivals, USA*. The other covered the Mamou run for *All Things Considered*. With enough time to develop the kinds of subtleties that the folklorist provided, the first report was satisfying in depth and accuracy. The second crew, on the other hand, "seemed to be looking for sound bites to illustrate a story they had basically developed by the time they arrived, based on the usual expectations of wildness and the *laissez le bon temps rouler* phenomenon. Basically they had a two or three minute package in mind and spent the whole day listening to the celebration through their earphones" (Spitzer 1985). Moreover, the *All Things Considered* crew apparently forgot that they were trying to work during play, which often puts journalists at odds with Mardi Gras participants. A female member of the second crew was especially riled by the macho nature of the Mamou celebration when at one point a band of masked horsemen surrounded her and forced her off the road. Spitzer later noted that she failed to consider that she was, first, a woman in a men's ritual and, second, an outsider asking probing questions during an insiders' ritual. The riders couldn't all articulate a response in her terms, so some had used their horses to communicate their feelings (Spitzer 1985).

A recurring problem among journalists covering the Mardi Gras is that they often don't seem to understand that they are being put on, in the very spirit of the day when they ask questions of the participants whose role for the day, they seem to forget, is to play the fool. In 1975 a crew called TVTV using experimental portable videotape cameras covered the Mamou Mardi Gras for a documentary called "The Good Times Are Killing Me" (Goldsmith et al. 1975). At one point the TVTV crew asked a group of children who were waiting for the Mardi Gras riders' return to town, "What kinds of things do you eat around here?" It is important to understand that Cajuns have parried scrutiny with irony and humor for generations. Practical joking is an integral part of their culture and they will go miles out of their way to put each other on (Ancelet 1984a: 107; Ancelet 1984b: 182–86). And outsiders fare no better (or worse), whether they understand it or not. Armed with a

Moss man, Mamou
Mardi Gras, 1996.
Photo by Donna
Onebane.

question about what they eat on any day of the year, many self-respecting Cajun kids would have jumped at the opportunity to play with its asker. Remember too that this is Mardi Gras day, on which playing the fool is not only acceptable but expected. True to their cultural heritage and to the spirit of the day, those children in Mamou spouted off a litany of foods that they felt would be bizarre and disgusting to outsiders, including squirrel heads, crawfish, and frogs.

The children on the streets of Mamou succeeded in "fooling" the documentary crew. The only problem was that the crew apparently didn't know that they had been "fooled" because they treated this information in their videotape as an anthropological discovery which reinforced their own stereotypes of the Cajuns. The TVTV crew used this information because the media generally perceives that people are interested in how other people are different. Even if they had recorded balancing statements that Cajuns also eat fried chicken and hamburgers, these remarks would likely have ended up on the cutting room floor because how people are the same is not as interesting. But what about the family in Nebraska watching PBS one night and hearing this list of foods with which they are unfamiliar and which they may consider to be grotesque? Did they know that there is "ordinary stuff" that was not used because it didn't illustrate the difference between Cajuns and themselves? Did they understand that it was Mardi Gras? Did they understand that Cajuns like to kid each other, and others? Or were they too in turn fooled? And what about the children at the Mardi Gras? They first succeeded in fooling the crew, but were they then fooled when the program aired creating second generation misinterpretations? And who is ultimately responsible for fooling the family in Nebraska? Should the children or other participants be expected to understand these issues, or should it be the journalists whose profession it is to analyze and interpret the facts?

Consider a similar example. In a 1985 article, *Time* blue highways-style reporter Gregory Jaynes quotes a Mamou Mardi Gras participant as saying, "See that boy dancing on that horse. . . . I never thought he'd be up this morning. Last night he was arrested for parking his horse in the wrong place. He thought he tied it to a parking meter but it was a fire hydrant" (14–15). The reader is not told that dancing on horseback is a common ritual exhibition of skill and machismo among Cajun cowboys during Mardi Gras. The jest about the horse tied to a fire hydrant Jaynes lets fend for itself. Without background information the whole incident comes across as bizarre, at best.

After taking a pot shot at the Cajuns' native language ("Cajun French has about as much in common with the French language as a claw hammer has with poetry"), Jaynes quotes another Mardi Gras rider for a "typical" example of Cajun English: "I told him for a job, he ask me no" (15), again assuming that the people he was interviewing were playing it straight when in fact that was exactly the opposite of their intention. They meant to fool him. But, again, who fooled

Church Point Mardi Gras, 2001. Dancing on horseback is part of the rural Mardi Gras tradition. Photo by Marcia Gaudet.

whom? After reading Jaynes's column, a woman from Flat Bush, New Jersey, wrote to the editor of *Time* that she was certainly happy that she didn't live in the Mamou that was described. The reaction to her comment among the folks in Mamou was generally that they were happy too that she did not live there if she couldn't even take a joke. In their minds the joke was on Jaynes and the lady from New Jersey. Among people across the rest of the country who took Jaynes's piece at face value, however, it seems clear that the joke was on Mamou. The remaining question is, where do reporters like Jaynes fit between Mamou and Flat Bush?

Even when journalists are in the spirit of things and understand the play involved, they sometimes don't successfully pass that information along to the audience, for whatever reason. For a definition of the Mardi Gras the TVTV crew asked a slightly drunk teenaged participant who offered, "Get drunk and have fun and dance. Get chickens. That's the meaning of Mardi Gras" (Goldsmith et al. 1975). Now it is certainly not reproachable to ask for the participant's point of view. However, at no time during the documentary did they balance the scales by interviewing Mardi Gras reviver and former Capitaine Paul Tate or current Capitaine Jasper Manual or any other informed source. Nor was the young Mardi Gras rider wrong. He could not be expected to wax eloquent on the deep meaning of the Mardi Gras from his point of view as a young initiate in the tradition.

Similarly, Jaynes offered the following assessment of what he learned in Mamou: "The lesson seemed to be: get drunk, hunt chickens, eat well, kiss the dickens out of pretty girls, straighten your deportment the next day, assume your place among your fellow men" (1985: 15), this despite talking to Mardi Gras organizer Paul Tate, Jr., who filled him in on the history and development of the tradition during a three-hour session at the Traveler's Café on Monday before Mardi Gras. Jaynes apparently passed little of this information on in his report. Tate, who unsuccessfully sued the *Washington Post* and reporter John Ed Bradley for allegedly misrepresenting him in a similar piece (Bradley 1984), thinks Jaynes was "distracted by other issues which shocked his East Coast liberal sensibilities, like the machismo of it all" (Tate 1985). Indeed he described the fights in much more detail than the costumes or the chicken chase. He seemed particularly preoccupied with the rule excluding women. According to Tate, Jaynes was upset because his girlfriend was not allowed to participate. Tate gave him several reasons including the fact that the women in Mamou were the ones who imposed and enforced the rule. All Jaynes used from that lengthy interview was a joke about the role of women that Tate flipped off as they were adjourning to Fred's Lounge (Tate 1985). In effect, Jaynes used his position at the typewriter to ridicule the culture's internal operatives, having failed to impose his own from the outside. He did not, however, reject the celebration wholesale. By his own admission, the alcohol he drank stained and strained his memory (1985: 14).

In one of its early sequences, just after giving a general introduction to Cajun culture, "The Good Times Are Killing Me" presents Louis Landreneau, a young man whose mother is helping him dress as a female nurse, a costume appropriate to the traditional Mardi Gras role reversal (rich and poor, male and female, etc.). Unfortunately the film has not introduced the Mardi Gras yet. The celebration has been cryptically suggested by extreme wide-angle close ups of a chicken with the Mardi Gras song as a sound-over. Consequently the sequence seems to represent a transvestite being dressed by his mother who calls him Louise. That impression is enhanced for the informal viewer by lines spoken in jest like "My mother always wanted a girl" and "I don't have a girlfriend right now," lines which any trained observer would recognize as Mardi Gras play. It is not until much later, when the Mardi Gras is formally introduced, that the viewer is given a clue that this might be part of a ritual. I wonder if the casual viewer can be expected to make such sophisticated deductions. The motives of the film crew must also be questioned here, especially since Mr. Landreneau protested specifically that he did not want the crew to use footage of him dressing because he feared that people would get the wrong idea (Landreneau 1975).

At another point in their film, this same TVTV crew betrayed its bias with a remarkable question and answer sequence. While following the Mardi Gras riders through the countryside, they happened on a farmer dressed in starched khakis watching the procession while standing by the side of the road in front of his house. Someone off camera asked, "What do you think about this?" leading to the following exchange:

"I've never run Mardi Gras before and if nothing happens, I'll never run."
"Why's that?"
"I don't like that. I'm glad [for] the ones that like it though. But me . . ."
"Why don't you like it?"
"Because I don't like to jump around all day like that. Then a fellow's got to drink if he wants to run Mardi Gras and it gets him sick the next day."
"Are you a Cajun?"
"Yeah, that's what I am."
"You don't sound like a Cajun."
"Why?"
"Most Cajuns like to run around and have a . . ."
"Yeah, most of them like to, but not me." (Goldsmith et al. 1975)

Mardi Gras in traditional wire screen mask and capuchon (right) with Mardi Gras example of role reversal (left), a young man playing the role of an "old woman." Photo by Donna Onebane.

The TVTV crew seemed genuinely shocked to find someone who didn't fit their notion of what a Cajun should be. The very next scene put things back into (their) perspective with drunk riders slurring the meaning of Mardi Gras.

Finally, the camera and tape recorder themselves are frequently overlooked factors in the relationship between the documenter and the documented. Pointing a lens or a microphone at people often makes ordinary folks act and speak in a self-conscious way. Some people feel uncomfortable in front of a camera and clam up. Others ham it up, overreacting for the record. These factors must be taken into account by the serious documenter when editing footage into a final story. TVTV, whose credits also include a special illustrating former President Gerald Ford's supposed clumsiness, may have misapplied their warts-and-all style of journalistic reporting to the documentation of a cultural event. Moreover, pointing a camera at a Mardi Gras rider whose goal is to play is all the cue he needs. This can lead to some very interesting performances, but it should be remembered that they are performances and not to be confused with reality.

An important part of the function of the Mardi Gras, of course, is to turn reality on its ear, making it difficult if not downright impossible to get a clear look at the host culture during this traditional festival. Yet journalists and filmmakers interested in documenting the Cajuns often schedule their visits to south Louisiana so that they will be able to cover the Mardi Gras as part of their research. In the worst cases these are on-the-road journalists who are primarily interested in grist for their "rube story" mills (Edmunds 1985). Even in the best of cases, however, many observers frequently come away with a distorted understanding of the culture in general because they forget to consider that they viewed it through a lens which is designed to distort. Often they base their reports on fascination rather than understanding. Sometimes they are even drawn into the festivities they are trying to observe and have to sift through beer-stained mental notes for information later. They rarely understand enough about the culture to know when they are being kidded and thus indiscriminately record stories meant to amuse. Unfortunately many go on to analyze the Mardi Gras only in terms of this misinformation and apparent foolishness. Those who expand this shaky analysis to use the Mardi Gras as a metaphor for the whole society confuse play with ordinary life and confuse their audiences as well in the bargain. Sadly this approach creates intercultural misunderstanding rather than the understanding we hope for as concerned folklorists.

References

Ancelet, Barry Jean. 1980. The Country Mardi Gras Celebration, *Attakapas Gazette* 15: 159–64.

———. 1984a. *The Makers of Cajun Music.* Austin: University of Texas Press.

———. 1984b. La Truie dans la brouette: Etude de la tradition orale en Louisiane francophone. Doctorat du 3e cycle dissertation. Etudes Creoles, Universite d'Aix Marseille I.

————. 1987. Mardi Gras. In *The Cajuns: Their History and Culture*, report to the Jean Lafitte National Historical Park and the National Park Service 2: 87–101.

Audet, Robert. 1982. *Mardi Gras Louisiane*. Film, 53 min. Cinequip Production.

Blank, Les. 1972. *Dry Wood*. Film, 37 min. Flower Films.

————. 1973. *Spend It All*. Film, 41 min. Flower Films.

Bradley, John Ed. 1984. Cajun Mardi Gras: The Native Returns for Raucous Rites. *Washington Post* 17 March.

Brim, Peggy, producer. 1978. The Mardi Gras They Couldn't Stop. Report on *20/20 News Magazine*, ABC Television.

Brunot, Jean-Pierre. 1973. *Dedans le sud de la Louisiane*. Film, 43 min. Bayou Films.

Edmunds, James. 1986. Personal interview.

Fishman, Mark. 1980. *Manufacturing the News*. Austin: University of Texas Press.

Goldsmith, Paul, et al. 1975. *The Good Times Are Killing Me*. Videotape, 58 min. TVTV.

Jaynes, Gregory. 1985. Louisiana: A Mad, Mad Mardi Gras. In American Scene. *Time* 125: 14–15.

Landreneau, Louis. 1975. Personal interview.

Lindahl, Carl. 1984. Bahktin and the Nature of Carnival Laughter. Unpublished typescript.

McCallum, Michael, et al. 1980. *Soileau Mardi Gras*. Videotape, 15 min. Crossover Productions.

Spitzer, Nicholas. 1985. Personal interview.

————. 1987. *Zydeco and Mardi Gras*. Report to the Jean Lafitte National Historical Park and the National Park Service.

Spitzer, Nicholas, and Stephen Duplantier. 1984. *Zydeco*. Film, 58 min. Bayou Films.

Tate, Paul, Jr. 1987. Personal interview.

2

Buffalo Bill and the Mardi Gras Indians

Michael P. Smith

The culture of New Orleans has always been characterized by the mixing and absorption of elements from many cultures. Most commonly acknowledged sources are the French, Spanish, African, Irish, Italian, and German. Sometimes, unexpected elements surface, such as the influence many scholars attribute to Mexican military bands whose instruments contributed to the development of jazz. One of the most unusual stories of all is the connection between the American West and our own Southern culture.

In 1884–85 New Orleans hosted the World's Industrial and Cotton Centennial Exposition—an event of international scope that brought culture and industry from many parts of the world to a feverish pitch of competition, borrowing, cross-fertilization, and synthesis. The Exposition, which lasted from December, 1884 until June, 1885, provided a lavish international festival atmosphere.

The Exposition was a very sophisticated trade exhibit with numerous international displays and interesting entertainments, including a large, racially integrated brass band that also played at various social clubs throughout the city. Many of the exhibits in the Exposition recognized the benefits of cultural diversity. There were separate exhibits for women and black Americans and frequent appearances of American Plains Indians, Mayan Indians, and other indigenous peoples, all in native costume. The Nevada Territory Exhibit also presented a respectful display of the art and culture of the American Plains Indians.

From *Cultural Vistas* (Fall 1992): 12–15, 34–37. Reprinted by permission of the author.

The Cotton Exposition, while it greatly enriched cultural interaction in the city, had its primary appeal in the literate community. Though heavily attended by blacks, the fair probably was visited more often by the established society, many of whom must have used the fair as an ongoing social event—much like New Orleanians utilized their 1984 World's Fair. The opening ceremonies of the Cotton Exposition set the exclusive tone featuring a Mardi Gras pageant presided over by Rex, King of Carnival, the figurehead of the establishment.

The Wild West Comes South

Of greater influence on the average New Orleanian—especially the less literate working classes and those who were not part of the predominant American society—was the Buffalo Bill Wild West Show. The Wild West Show wintered in New Orleans in 1884–85 and performed regularly, over a four-month period, before large crowds in a popular multi-ethnic recreation area known as Oakland Park and Riding Stables, a cheap trolley ride and short walk from the foot of Canal Street. This show was attended repeatedly by minority, working-class people.

A grand parade publicizing the opening of the Wild West Show in New Orleans on December 22, 1884, left Oakland Park (the present site of the New Orleans Country Club) at about 10 A.M., marched up Canal Street to St. Charles, Washington, Magazine, Calliope, Camp, Canal, Rampart, Esplanade, Royal, Canal, and then back to Oakland Park. A reporter for *The Daily Picayune*, describing the opening ceremonies, referred to "an onslaught of a whole band of whooping red-devils. . . . The Indians wore their semicivilized garb, were gorgeous in their native war paint and spoke their own guttural language . . . and they went through the weird dances of their race." The impact of this magnificent street theater, including "costumed and armed Plains warriors, some of them perhaps recent victors over Custer, striding proudly through the streets of New Orleans," obviously left a lasting impression on blacks and other minority ethnic groups in the city.

Although news coverage of the Wild West Show was sparse compared to coverage of the Cotton Exposition, *The Daily Picayune* judged the show "as interesting as anything to be seen at the Exposition," and regularly noted increasing attendance. Of the two extravaganzas, the Wild West Show was "the people's choice." By March 1885 *The Daily Picayune* was reporting the show as "such a show of novelties and sensations as can be seen nowhere else in the world." In spite of inclement weather throughout that spring, *The Daily Picayune* made numerous references to "large crowds" at the show.

Buffalo Bill portrayed and marketed the myth of white supremacy and social Darwinism. The pageant depicted the Anglo-Saxon "manifest destiny" and graphically represented the conquest of the Plains Indians—already a mythic people among blacks. One Wild West program referred to the white/ Indian conflict as part of America's pursuit of "the Anglo Saxon's commercial necessities" and summed up with the definitive statement: "the inevitable law of survival of the fittest had to determine who would control 'nature's cornucopia.'" "Fittest," of course, meant superior guns and numbers. In sum, the Wild West Show promoted the idea that white America was divinely commissioned to be its "brother's keeper."

Black cowboys worked in all of the Wild West shows that toured during that era, and must have developed lasting friendships with the Plains Indians and other ethnic groups in the shows. According to the Buffalo Bill Museum in Cody, Wyoming, there was at least one black cowboy and a large number of black cowhands in the Buffalo Bill Wild West show. There were also five major ethnic groups that traveled and worked together in the show—including Chinese, Mexicans, blacks, whites, and Indians. At times the international cast included "Russian cossacks, Turkish bedouins, Argentine gauchos, Mexican vaqueros, and French Chasseurs. . . . In later years when the Wild West dramatized historical events they hired Cubans, Filipinos, Hawaiians, and Chinese."

Despite the relative exclusiveness of the Cotton Exposition and despite any manifest destiny and white supremacy messages imbedded in the Wild West Show, both were models of cultural diversity and pan-ethnic industry. The actual working and living environments of the Wild West Show, in particular, resembled the permeability of early French colonial society in New Orleans, and might well have functioned in much the same way.

Rooting for the Victim

African-Americans were surely in sympathetic contact with the Plains Indians in New Orleans during all those months. Given the sense of Anglo-Saxon superiority conveyed in the show, the explicit supremacy message carried in the show program, and worsening racial conditions in New Orleans at that time, blacks were given ample reason to reconsider their own circumstances and future.

The great majority of common folk in New Orleans would have condemned the genocide portrayed and would have ridiculed the white supremacy notion carried by the show. Blacks who attended the Buffalo Bill Wild West Show would have sympathized with the Indians rather than with Buffalo Bill, and would have departed the show identifying strongly with the Indians' struggle.

Knowing well the vernacular, multicultural character of the modern city, and having attended "Cowboy-and-Indian" movies in black neighborhoods myself—where the attending public heartily supports the Indians rather than the cowboys— I would suspect that the show focused attention on the plight of blacks and Indians together as outcast peoples threatened by a common enemy—white chauvinism and America's "Christian" interest in reshaping the world in the mold of Anglo-American civilization.

Mardi Gras in New Orleans in 1885 was extraordinary. On the streets were large numbers of international visitors connected with the Exposition, a number of Central American Indian groups from Mexico, and some fifty to sixty Plains

Indians from the Wild West Show, including four chiefs, all of whom were likely on the streets of the city, at some point, in their native ceremonial dress.

Such an unusual celebration of community, creative imagination, and international camaraderie—all within the revolutionary "devil may care," "in your face," "anything can happen" context of the New Orleans Mardi Gras—must have been both an inspiring occasion for the black leaders, and a nightmarish vision for the white supremacists.

Masking Indian

According to the oral tradition of some present-day Mardi Gras Indian gangs, a number of Afro-New Orleanians masked as Indians on that occasion. We will never know the exact social dynamics involved, but Mardi Gras presented a wonderful opportunity to celebrate multiculturalism and the ancient friendship between blacks and Indians. "Masking Indian" in large tribal formations soon became a recognizable part of Mardi Gras.

Ironically, the designation "Mardi Gras Indian" has become a mask in itself. That superficial identification made in the last century now spurs widespread confusion about just who or what the "Mardi Gras Indians" are. Today that label is used in the outside community and in the popular press with little understanding, eclipsing the identity of one of America's most important cultural heritages—a traditional African-American heritage, little changed in New Orleans over the past 250 or more years, which continues all year around and is only incidentally connected with Mardi Gras or American Indians.

These societies are more properly described, perhaps, as the Maroons of Urban New Orleans. Maroons were among the first Americans to resist colonial domination, striving for independence, forging new cultures and identities, and developing solidarity out of diversity. In the French colony of Saint-Domingue, maroons helped to launch the Haitian Revolution, which gave birth to one of the first independent republics in the Americas in 1804. The music, dance, verbal arts, and spiritual traditions of contemporary Maroon peoples remain the carriers of a rich heritage that came to New Orleans initially during the French and Spanish colonial period, and descends in large part from the early Afro-Creole population of the city. Now long submerged in the inner city, their identity obscured by the processes of racism and simplistic definition by outsiders, the "Mardi Gras Indians" pursue cultural traditions rooted in what they know only as a mysterious past, their own history being little known beyond its vibrant oral tradition.

Despite being some fifteen to twenty generations removed from its original source in Africa, and despite severe oppression, this culture serves to instill a deep-seated ethnic pride in the black community, and continues to maintain individual spirits against the demoralizing effects of modern urbanization and ghettoization.

Everything going on in the city in 1885 would have sensitized the community to such an exhibition and made this sort of cross-cultural activity highly visible and more likely to be commented upon and remembered. In former times, underclass groups, or Afro-Indian tribal groups, could have marched the back streets of the city—going to or coming from Congo Square or other meeting places—without being noted in the historical record. Locals would have considered these goings on to be either too mundane or too déclassé to write about unless it led to some disturbance.

The commonly accepted history of present-day Mardi Gras Indian gangs begins at just about that time. The first such gang usually considered to be in the Mardi Gras Indian tradition was named the "Creole Wild West"—presumably as a carnivalesque reference to the Buffalo Bill Wild West Show. This gang was founded sometime around 1885 by Becate Batiste, a Seventh Ward Creole of African-American, French, and Choctaw heritage.

Variance of Style

Among the several styles of African-American Indian Carnival masking in New Orleans, one source of the Amerindian motif thus seems clear. But there is much more to the "Mardi Gras Indians" than groups that adopted a Plains Indians dress style. Different "carnivalesque" groups dressed in different ways. Some dressed like the maskers and dancers during the Carnival period in 1781, who were banned because of their "exhibitions against the public quietness." Some dressed like revelers during Carnival in 1823: "For a crown he has a series of oblong, gilt paper boxes on his head, tapering upwards, like a pyramid." Other gangs followed in the path of "Native American militia" described in accounts from 1836. There were different styles for different periods, but the cultural pattern and substance remained the same.

The abstract, sculptural style of dress is more typical of "downtown" Indians. "Uptown" gangs follow the American Indian style of dress, featuring elaborate beaded, pictorial scenes—now usually "Cowboy-and-Indian" visions of the American West. This uptown/downtown difference can be found in tribal music styles and organization, as well as in costume design, sewing styles, and materials used. These variations continue today—though the uptown/downtown distinction is becoming increasingly "muddied" at this point.

It is likely that the source of these differences can be found in the origins of the two communities. In general the downtown Creole community descended largely from the Senegambian peoples who came to New Orleans during the French and Spanish colonial periods. The uptown black community, on the other hand, came to New Orleans in three great waves: from the Caribbean islands (from Haiti via Cuba, largely in 1809), from the "Old South" plantations on the eastern seaboard during the "Americanization" period (English-speaking slaves), and from the Louisiana plantations after the Civil War (mainly Creole-speaking slaves).

With respect to the groups arriving from the Caribbean, dress styles in New Orleans would certainly have been influenced by the "roots" and "fancy dress" concepts carried here from the West Indies by members of Jonkonnu, Rara, and other groups.

Other Influences

As for the American Plains Indians connection, it should also be considered that shortly after the Civil War hundreds of freed slaves had been induced to join the U.S. Ninth Cavalry Regiment (the "Buffalo Soldiers") and were shipped West to fight the Plains Indians. Some of these soldiers must have returned to New Orleans in later years as cowboys and roustabouts in the employment of numerous Wild West shows and carnivals. Their Army experience would have hardened their perceptions of what might be expected from "American" rule. They might well have concluded that only through multicultural alliances would they have any hope for freedom. Blacks working in the Wild West shows became friends with the Plains Indians and both must have socialized with and influenced the underclass populations of each community visited by the traveling shows.

A large number of traveling Wild West shows visited the city during the late nineteenth and early twentieth centuries. Among others were a Mexican Wild West Show at the Fair Grounds, The Hagenback Wallace Creole Wild West Show, the 101 Traveling Wild West Show from the "101 Ranch" in Oklahoma, and an African Wild West Show, which played to large audiences in the Gentilly area around the turn of the century.

The 101 Wild West Show, like many of these shows, had a full complement of black cowboys, and various admixtures of blacks, whites, Seminole Indians and Cherokee Indians. There was also a Mardi Gras Indian gang, dating from the same period, named the "101 Wild West" gang, giving additional substance to the idea that traveling carnival shows influenced the expression of African American culture in New Orleans.

Surely the effects of industrial trade shows, small carnivals, itinerant tent shows, minstrel and vaudeville shows, and various Wild West shows on society and politics in New Orleans during this period were much greater and more complex than historians have recognized to date.

It was during this period, the last two decades of the nineteenth century, and in just these sorts of vibrant, multicultural environments that information was communicated into the black community about what really happened at Little Big Horn and Wounded Knee, and exactly what Crazy Horse, Sitting Bull, Geronimo, and Black Hawk were fighting about . . . not as reported in the establishment press, but what was being said among common working-class peoples in the environments of the various traveling shows. These opinions, of course, would have been very different from those in the established Anglo-American society. Many of these folk oriented entertainments traveled internationally and served as vehicles for diverse cultural communications between various societies— much like musicians employed in the shipping trades who cross-fertilized the music worlds of the great port cities. It was information and ideas gained through national and international travel that informed the popular movement against the elitist, Anglo-American hegemony . . . and for the wide-open, heterogeneous, multicultural Creole society in New Orleans, which, at this point, was giving birth to music later known as jazz.

Further division between the "high" and "low" communities was being caused by the implications of Custer's "last stand," which had occurred just a few years before (1876). It could be said that the Americans were not invincible, that the blacks and Indians, if they combined their forces, might be an unbeatable combination. It was a time of great fear and polarization in America.

New Orleans by the 1890s was becoming harshly segregated on the basis of a pathological color line dictated by Anglo-Protestant Americans . . . "one drop of African blood" determined one's identification as black. This attitude, reinforced by law in 1893, produced an almost intolerable situation for a large part of the population of New Orleans which was either reduced to "passing" as white or to accepting the loss of basic human rights.

Just a few short years after the close of the Buffalo Bill Wild West Show and the Cotton Exposition the lid clamped tight on black society. Jim Crow laws banned blacks from public parks, and enforced the strictest segregation in all public facilities. Vernacular black culture (especially the "savage" and "dangerous" sort most repugnant to radical whites such as that of the Mardi Gras Indians) retreated deep into the neighborhoods and back streets of the city. It would not be seen or reported again, practically speaking, for almost another century. This is not to say that it did not continue as a living culture serving the interior community, but it is to say that it was denied recognition and support by the city of its birth.

3

Every Man a King

Worldview, Social Tension, and
Carnival in New Orleans

Frank de Caro and Tom Ireland

Public celebrations and public performances are enacted
because they have "meanings" for those who enact them.
They communicate ideas, beliefs and feelings and may often
constitute complex symbol systems designed to interconnect
attitudes and emotions. The complexity of such systems may
be considerable, especially if the celebration itself is multifac-
eted, and individual participants in a given celebration may,
of course, be aware of only limited aspects of the celebration's total significance. There may be public statements of
the event's meaning which only partially explain it or which
may even conflict with private understandings. Even a community as a whole may not fully understand the event's
nature and significance, part of which may lie at a level of
structure only subliminally appreciated. The full meaning of
the celebration may be understood only after considerable
analysis which attempts to examine carefully and interpret all
of the relevant elements. Such attempts at analysis of public
celebrations in American culture include Warner's interpreta-
tion of Memorial Day and Grimes's book-length study of the
Santa Fe Fiesta.[1] The present chapter attempts an analysis of
Carnival celebrations in New Orleans, a series of events commonly referred to as Mardi Gras, though technically Mardi
Gras (meaning Fat Tuesday) refers only to the final day of the
celebration, which is a season stretching from 6 January,
Twelfth Night, to the Tuesday before Ash Wednesday, the
beginning of the religious season of Lent. Activity intensifies

---

From *International Folklore Review* 6 (1988): 58–66. Reprinted by permission of the authors.

over the weekend preceding Mardi Gras, and Fat Tuesday itself is an especially powerful culmination, with tens of thousands of people, many in costume, gathered together for several parades.

Carnival is indeed a complex celebration. It is celebrated in different ways by different people and these differences are drawn partly along class and ethnic boundary lines. The Carnival season in part structures the social season of the city's élites, for example in terms of débutantes being "presented" to "society" at this time. Various aspects of the Carnival season range along a spectrum from very private to totally public. For example, the celebration may be the focus for intimate family reunions, as natives who have left New Orleans commonly return home periodically for the festivities. On the other hand, the famous parades are witnessed by thousands and thousands, including many tourists who may have no other connection with the Carnival season. In the present chapter we shall discuss a number of facets of Carnival, including aspects of its historical development, but our focus will be upon two elements, the parades and the balls. We are concerned primarily with the symbolic structure of each, which we see as pointing to the basic underlying function and meaning of Carnival as a whole.

In studying, respectively, Memorial Day and the Santa Fe Fiesta, Warner and Grimes examined occasions very different in terms of their outward forms—one a solemn national holiday honouring the nation's war dead, the other a local series of events combining the solemn and the festive and celebrating local history and feelings. No doubt the participants in these two occasions have feelings quite different from each other, and there can be no doubt that the atmosphere which influences and is created by each occasion is unlike that of the other. Yet both Warner and Grimes find through examinations of two very unlike systems of symbols that both celebrations have at their hearts a very similar function—the creation of social unity. Warner contends that Memorial Day unifies an America and individual American communities where there are "conflicting symbols and opposing, autonomous churches and associations."[2] Grimes sees the Santa Fe Fiesta as symbolically fusing together civic and religious elements in a society officially secular but in which Roman Catholicism plays a major role, and ethnic elements in a society which is "officially" said to be one of bicultural harmony but in which there has in fact been historical conflict and continuing tension between Indian, Hispanic and Anglo groups.[3] We suggest that the New Orleans Carnival plays a similar role in unifying different groups and conflicting world views.

We do not, of course, mean to imply that this is the only function of Carnival. The New Orleans celebration fits into a larger European and New World tradition of pre-Lenten carnival with the declared purpose of such events being to provide a period of feasting and license before the penitential season of Lent. New Orleans has been and still is a very Catholic city and Mardi Gras has provided just such a prepenitential bacchanal; traditionally at least, Mardi Gras activities end sharply at midnight with the beginning of Ash Wednesday. There is also the aspect of individual masking—that is, the donning of costumes, though a mask or other method of face disguising is commonly a part of this—which allows people to act out private fantasies and to assume non-normal roles:

> You use the costume as a disguise, so that nobody knows you're John Doe—you're Bozo the Clown, or you're [a] He-Man, and you can take on those characteristics. . . . If you're inhibited, you can flash people on Mardi Gras and nobody knows who you are and you've turned yourself around and become something you have not allowed yourself to do before. It's a good outlet for open expression.[4]

Role change and role reversal are, of course, an important facet of other carnival celebrations, as well as of other festivals, such as the Hindu Holi celebration. But we maintain that the symbolic unification of groups and attitudes is one fundamental purpose of Carnival in New Orleans, a purpose that is shared with at least one other New World carnival, that of Trinidad, of which Errol Hill has written: "Ethnic and social division in multicolored Trinidad society are submerged under a national will to make each successive carnival 'the greatest ever!' "[5]

Various commentators upon New Orleans Carnival have noted relationships between the celebration and New Orleans society and culture as a whole. Munro Edmonson has written, for example:

> [Carnival] reflects its [New Orleans's] complex society and social differentiation. From an examination of the Mardi Gras festivities . . . we may infer a great deal about New Orleans's view of itself as a city and about the attitudes and values of various groups of its people.[6]

In his study of the Mardi Gras Indians, Draper seconds such observations by noting that "the Mardi Gras season, as a ritualistic drama, provides a public statement of the social structure of New Orleans."[7] The poet and novelist Ishmael Reed, half tongue in cheek, has suggested structural similarities between Mardi Gras and New Orleans voodoo.[8] Professional artists in the Crescent City have contended that they cannot make a living there because so much local artistic energy and interest go not into buying their works of art but into expressing creativity through costly Carnival costumes and activities. And, indeed, many Orleanians are quite aware that kinds of participation in Mardi Gras relate to power and status and presume that certain Carnival organizations play a role in interconnecting members of local élites, an aspect investigated by the sociologist Phyllis Raabe. Raabe concluded that Carnival is indeed an important mechanism for upper-class status and, though it is hardly the only factor in determining such status, it provides "an added and elaborate differentiating mechanism."[9] It can be "a source of class identity" and bolster upper-class conservatism and dominance.[10]

An upper-class dominance of Carnival activities is something of which most Orleanians are at least vaguely aware ("If you are of foreign descent—say, black, Oriental, Hispanic— you're not going to belong to any of the krewes."[11]) and something which commentators upon the celebration have certainly noted. Edmonson has written: "There can be little doubt that the main ideological content of Carnival is aristocratic."[12] The principal krewes—that is, Carnival organizations which hold parades and balls—have members drawn from the upper classes and these organizations are very exclusive indeed. Their membership tends to be limited to what Edmonson calls the "Anglo-French upper class" [13]—though that term must be construed somewhat loosely—and persons from the more newly arrived ethnic groups, in the recent past particularly Jews and Italians, have been largely excluded from membership. Certainly these krewes are all white organizations. The Carnival balls, especially the Comus ball, are the highlights of the upper-class social season.

Interesting also is the symbolism we see worked out in the parades and balls. A Carnival parade basically consists of floats pulled by tractors (at one time horses, later mules), the floats elaborately decorated and collectively expressing some theme, often drawn from fantasy, fairy tales or history. The king of the krewe, chosen annually from among the members, rides upon a throne on the first float, carrying a scepter and waving to the crowd. There are also a few support vehicles and a few krewe officials who ride horses, while the great majority of krewe members ride the floats. High school or military bands are periodically interspersed to provide music. For a night parade there may also be flambeau carriers. Throughout the parade the krewe members dispense "throws" to the crowd—that is, they toss out favours, particularly strings of plastic (until recently glass) beads and since 1960 aluminum coins called doubloons, which are specially minted each year.

The symbolism of the parade is fairly obvious. Here are beautifully dressed aristocrats, physically raised above the multitude, riding through the populace either on horseback or on exquisite, expensive vehicles, throwing bits of their riches to the clamouring mob. Not only do they dispense wealth, but they are also providing—*noblesse oblige*—a spectacle to entertain the masses; thus they perform a sort of public drama within the larger public drama which includes another group of actors. Those actors, the ground-level participants— one cannot really call them spectators—become beggars fawning upon the aristocrats for their largesse, and indeed they *do* clamour for the throws. The eagerness with which parade attenders chase trinkets, stepping on other people's grasping hands, pushing small children and grandmothers aside, is well known Carnival lore. The traditional Carnival cry of the groundlings—"Hey, t'row me something, mister"— further emphasizes their beggary and suggests also lower-class dialect. For at least one middle-aged avid Carnival participant this symbolic division at the parades has become part of his personal historical vision of Carnival: "You know, the whole idea [of] Mardi Gras . . . started with the nobility or rich of New Orleans giving to the poor. The ruling class was on the floats and the crowd on the streets was the peasants."[14] The masks through which the float riders look down upon the masses are commonly regarded as arrogant. And for the night parades the flambeau carriers add another note of class distinction. Flambeaux are traditional, very heavy torches, used today by only one or two of the most exclusive krewes; they are carried by lower-class blacks, who thus assume the role of a servant class, a role which of course blacks commonly fill in New Orleans social reality. Because of the weight and awkwardness of the flambeaux, these carriers assume a sort of stooped, shuffling gait, a manner of walking often associated with Negro subservience.

Carnival balls also take a unique form. The most striking feature of these balls—one that often amazes those who first learn of it—is that invited guests are generally not permitted to dance. Most balls are held at the Municipal Auditorium on the edge of the French Quarter and hold to a general pattern. A ball opens with a tableau, which is followed by the entrance of the queen (a débutante) and her court. She is greeted by the king of the krewe and there is a grand march with the dukes of the krewe escorting the queen's maids. There may also be at some point a presentation of the previous year's queen and probably also a presentation of prominent guests. Dancing begins and follows a distinctive pattern. Members of the krewe, who are masked, are the only male dancers; they obtain partners from among the female invited guests through the "call out" system. Members of a floor committee, who are not in costume but in full dress, locate those who are invited to dance and escort them to their masked partners on the floor.

Thus male invited guests do not get to dance at all and the same is in fact true for many female guests, for krewe members are allotted a limited number of call outs and these must be used to some extent by the year's débutantes.

This may seem an absurd situation—not only a dance where invited guests do not get to dance, but one to which to be invited at all is considered a great social honour. But again the symbolism is striking. Again a strict sense of hierarchy is emphasized. There is all the panoply of royalty and a royal court with its various strata: king, queen, dukes, maids of honour, functionaries and ordinary dancing nobility. And there are those who are mere spectators, their lack of costume emphasizing that they are not of the courtly class. Though certainly of higher status than the parade groundlings, they too are watching another public drama—a fact emphasized by the opening tableau conspicuously put on by a higher class. They surely are the lesser gentry or perhaps the bourgeoisie looking on admiringly at their social betters, linked to them by the temporary "exchange" of their non-costumed débutante women.

The aristocratic tenor of Mardi Gras can be read in other signs as well. On Mardi Gras night, for example, Rex, king of the krewe of Rex, who is also the titular king of Carnival as a whole, ritually meets the king of Comus, the oldest and most exclusive krewe. However, Rex goes to visit Comus, a fact which has been interpreted "to mean that the monarch of the city-wide Carnival privately acknowledges the supremacy of the aristocratic upper classes."[15] And there are anecdotes which stress this also. In one narrative a woman from an old New Orleans family who is married to a Jew receives a ball invitation addressed to her alone; and of course she goes, alone. Another story involves the year an important krewe had a float with a number of moving parts. Inside the float were several black boys hired to work by hand the machinery which drove those parts. During the parade the krewe members riding on the float found that they could slip inside this particular float and have a place to urinate down into the darkness below (though many floats are today equipped with portable toilets, this has not always been the case). They later discovered that they had spent the entire parade urinating on the heads of the boys working the machinery. Though this story was told to one of us to express an important Carnival anxiety—much drinking and a shortage of toilets creates problems—it is difficult to not see the symbolism of aristocrats blithely peeing all over their inferiors.

However, if the symbolic pattern of Carnival, or at least of major aspects of Carnival, emphasizes class divisions, hierarchy, superiors lording it over inferiors, we may well ask how the celebration has managed to continue. Why does it not exacerbate tension and result in social dysfunction? Why do the great mass of people continue to participate in a festival which turns them into clamouring peasants literally looked down upon by their betters? Why do the "non-aristocrats" who are consciously aware of the "aristocratic tone" of the celebration continue to go along with it? Indeed, not all do. There are New Orleans residents who ignore the celebration, a few who even make it a point to leave town at Mardi Gras time. Letters have appeared in local newspapers decrying the exclusionary aspects and one local columnist has even suggested, tongue somewhat in cheek, that Mardi Gras may be unconstitutional.[16] Yet the great majority of the population go on celebrating with gusto. In explaining this we cannot ignore the fact that Carnival is more than the great statement of hierarchical division we have suggested—it allows for license and individual and small-group fantasies, for example. And Edmonson suggests that such mass participation is also the result of widespread local belief in "the glamour of the Old South, and of Creole times and a general adherence to a local tradition conceived of as romantic."[17]

Such explanations do not seem to be entirely adequate, however, and we wish to suggest that in fact Carnival both acts as an acknowledgment of New Orleans class and caste structure and also serves as a statement that the social tension inherent in such a structure is subject to mediation not only by local forces but also by a national ethos which is ultimately greater than the regional one. The aspects of Mardi Gras which we have described to some degree reflect New Orleans society. There is an old-line élite; there is still considerable concern with social status. Informants have suggested to us that the élite is still very conservative and close-knit and closed to certain ethnic groups and, indeed, to newcomers in general. Some Orleanians express fears that continued progress will bypass the Crescent City as outside businesses hesitate to relocate there because their executives will be shut out of certain social power centers. Certainly there is ongoing racial division. On one level Carnival does emphasize hierarchy and social division. Yet in other ways it serves to break such divisions down and to mock their very existence. This it does in several ways, though in essence it is a matter of the celebration's simply being fluid enough to allow anyone to appropriate the central symbols and/or to allow outgroups to establish within the general festival their own range of symbolic behavior.

The latter course is that which has been taken by some New Orleans blacks. This is not surprising in that blacks have been traditionally at the bottom of the local social hierarchy and even in some ways excluded from public Carnival activities—for example, at one time they were not permitted to wear masks. The two most public ways in which they have responded to Carnival is through the Zulu Social Aid and Pleasure Club and the Black Indian Tribes.

The Indian tribes are neighbourhood-based associations governed by a Big Chief. The mostly male members parade through the streets on Mardi Gras Day, following no fixed route, dressed in elaborate "Indian" costumes which each member makes for himself every year. These costumes are vaguely Plains Indian in style, replete with multitudes of yellow or blue or pink feathers in the headdresses and including intricate beadwork. A tribe will march, often from bar to bar, keeping a look-out for other tribes, singing traditional songs. When another tribe is encountered there is war—in terms of boasting, flaunting of finery and ritual dance combat (though at one time actual fighting was apparently common and it is said that some Indians still carry concealed weapons).[18]

The Zulu parade is somewhat more akin to the white parades, though there are significant differences. Traditionally—and this pattern has changed in the last few years—the Zulu parade kept to only a loosely fixed route and included numerous stops at saloons and funeral parlours in black neighborhoods. King Zulu and his court would arrive from the river on a barge and there would be rudimentary floats. Zulu members are decked out in "African" garb—which includes grass skirts, spears and shields—and their faces are blackened with white makeup used to heighten certain parts of the face, especially the eyes. They also wear long black underwear and black "woolly wigs."[19] For throws they toss (or in recent years hand out) highly sought after coconuts.

What blacks have done in these instances is to substitute their own expressive systems for that of white-dominated Carnival involvement, also, in the case of Zulu, parodying white Mardi Gras and white conceptions. The Indians are in part engaging in a form of protest and are aware of their black identity. Members of the tribes consciously admire the warlike spirit of real Indians and are aware of Indian resistance to white domination; also, the inclusion of a white member in one tribe for several recent years has occasioned keen resentment on the part of other tribes. On another level, however, the Indians are clearly abandoning their black identity to become in fantasy the members of another racial group. They are thus simultaneously affirming the reality of their social position and negating that reality by assuming the role of a group which is largely irrelevant to New Orleans social structure, a group—Indians—which also has high status in the American imagination. They thus become liminal figures who render irrelevant the hierarchy established by other aspects of Carnival.

Zulu does something similar through its use of a burlesque African stereotype. The blackening of already "black" skin, the grass skirts and spears, the woolly wigs, the use of makeup to suggest large white eyes and thick lips all play upon the white physical stereotype of the Negro and mental stereotype of his African savagery. Thus the existence of the stereotype is acknowledged but also parodied and made ridiculous, the Carnival occasion allowing for a mocking repudiation of the social position associated with the damning stereotype. In part Zulu also parodies white Mardi Gras—a king, floats, throws—thus aiming satire directly at the white symbolic structure, marking its ridiculousness, and providing a (distorted) mirror image substitute for the black community.

If blacks symbolically deal with the hierarchical structure of white Mardi Gras by providing alternative performance structures, those whites who are excluded from the aristocracy—ethnics and others not of the social élite, as well as women, for the krewes are essentially male organizations—do so simply by appropriating the élite symbols. They have formed their own krewes with their own parades, their own kings and queens, and their own balls, constituting themselves into aristocracy parading before the masses just as the older, more exclusive krewes do. There are now dozens of parades during the Carnival season and in particular the number of Carnival organizations in middle-class suburbs has grown. Recent years have also seen the rise to prominence of the krewe of Bacchus. Said to have been founded by *nouveaux riches* denied entry to the older organizations, Bacchus has established an immensely popular and especially lavish night parade and features a celebrity such as Perry Como or Henry Winkler as king. Moreover, the organization sells tickets to its ball, which is open to virtually anyone who can pay. Other Carnival participants choose to join one of the two "truck parades" which follow the Rex parade on Mardi Gras Day and are open to all comers. They do so in groups of friends, relatives and neighbours by creating a single float on a flatbed truck; each float follows a theme and the riders mask in costumes to match. Although there is no king and no ball to follow, the riders throw trinkets to the crowd as they pass.

Certainly all of these actions can be seen as symbolic counter-statements to the aristocratic dominance of Carnival. The fact that "anyone" (though of course not literally anyone) can assume the trappings and behavior patterns of aristocracy and kingship renders meaningless the very idea of aristocracy, which of course on one level exists only as a Carnival fantasy to begin with. It is a case of "every man a king,"[20] at least in the sense that the potential for royal status is open to comparatively large numbers of people and that every Mardi Gras season has dozens of kings and queens floating about—a situation which stresses equality rather than hierarchy: kingship itself is so fluid that "anyone" can assume it. In one sense King Bacchus is the ultimate statement of this idea. Though that position is always filled by a national celebrity and hence not open to "anyone," this celebrity is by definition an outsider to the New Orleans social structure. Thus even a stranger to the *polis*, a liminal figure, can be raised to the kingship—a statement which flies against the idea of the Carnival king as coming from the native upper classes and another factor undermining the pretensions to exclusiveness of that office. The truck floats undermine the aristocratic tone of Mardi Gras in another way. Their spatial temporal position in the Mardi Gras parade is a secondary one, thus on one level affirming the hierarchical symbolism. But their presence in the parade affirms that anyone can be up there elevated above the crowd and throwing riches as they pass by, even people who do not have kings and queens and dukes, who do not affect the arrogant masks of the krewe maskers, whose parade themes are more likely to revolve around punning word play or popular culture than the exalted literary or historical themes of the krewe parades, and whose composition is not limited to one sex or age group but rather includes, democratically, men, women and children. The fact that the truck float riders are widely perceived as being more generous with their throws than krewe float riders suggests an undermining of the idea of aristocratic wealth. Finally, we must of course note that everyone who participates in Carnival is ultimately aware of the fluidity of the aristocrat-groundling dichotomy. The person who is riding a float one day may be scrambling for trinkets the next and the families and friends of lofty aristocrats are down in the crowd. The duke at one ball may become the nondancing spectator at another. The fantasy roles are freely switched.

What we are maintaining, then, is that Carnival symbolically mediates between two opposing social ideals: that of kingship, aristocracy and class hierarchy on the one hand; that of equality on the other. The aristocratic tone of the celebration is obvious, but close analysis shows that this tone is decisively tempered. In so far as Carnival mirrors New Orleans society—and it does to some extent, not that there are any real kings or queens—we see a celebration in the context of which the local élite is allowed to assert its social dominance and exclusiveness, yet in which that dominance is also challenged and shown to be ultimately meaningless, compromised by other local forces and by a larger national ideal of social equality. The fusing of the expressions of these two opposing "worldviews" into a single great celebration dispels a basic contradiction in local social attitudes by preserving but also partially obliterating social divisions and simultaneously by channeling the energies of members of diverse social groups towards a common purpose in a common arena in which élite and non-élite can accommodate each other and thus come together in harmony. Social tension is eased in an atmosphere of goodwill, a process which may carry over beyond Carnival itself, for New Orleans is a city with a history of contention between groups over political, social and cultural dominance: French versus Spanish, Creole versus American, French language versus English language, slave versus free, black versus white, uptown versus downtown, Yankee versus Confederate, perhaps even local versus tourist. Indeed, the two opposing worldviews we have detailed above may stem from fundamental developments in New Orleans history.

One intense division in New Orleans history, one which continues to the present day in only fairly small ways, is that which began early in the nineteenth century when Louisiana became part of the United States. There was an influx of Americans into New Orleans and a powerful influx of American culture and influence, which was strongly resisted by the French-speaking Creoles, who attempted to remain aloof from the newcomers and who in fact avoided selling them property in the French Quarter, a factor which occasioned the development of an American sector of the city, the Garden District. It at least seems quite possible that the opposing worldviews we have discussed above stem from this particular period of cultural and political conflict. We do not mean to imply that class consciousness and snobbery are unique to Creole society and of course today's élite contains many of Anglo-Saxon ancestry. But Creole society was royalist, colonialist, hierarchical, status-conscious, socially rigid in many ways, sharing in a larger French Catholic worldview which emphasized hierarchy too. The hierarchical, aristocratic side of Carnival may in part be a legacy and a survival of Creole society. On the other hand, the advancing Americans would have brought with them an ethos of equality and at least the ideal of little tolerance for uppity social pretensions, the other side of the Carnival coin.

The celebration of Mardi Gras is of course a French tradition carried on in Louisiana, but the form of present day Mardi Gras was in fact established by Anglo-Saxons from Mobile (where Carnival is also celebrated), who founded Comus in 1857. The fact of Anglo-Saxons' establishing what we have termed the aristocratic pattern of parades and balls might at first seem to indicate that this aspect could hardly be a Creole legacy—indeed, initially the Creoles shunned this form of Mardi Gras. But it is fairly well established that this form of Mardi Gras came about as an attempt to ease social tensions, those caused by the increasing rowdiness of the earlier type of celebration, such as street masking that erupted into fights and balls which were often crashed by the drunken uninvited. In the 1850s,

> Carnival continued to fall into disrepute. . . . Newspapers joined . . . in denouncing it as having become increasingly disreputable. The Creoles blamed it on the Americans, and the Americans blamed the Creoles. It is true that the festivities were becoming more and more rowdy. There was much drunkenness and fighting and subsequent filling of jails. "Licentiousness reigned again," was about all the *Daily Delta* said of the celebration of 1856.[21]

The early Comus parade provided a dignified and controlled focus. It seems logical to suppose that this form of Carnival was also introduced, though perhaps not so consciously, to ease other tensions, those between Creoles and Americans. By accepting and revitalizing a French tradition the Americans were signaling a rapprochement between the two groups and before long the Creoles were joining in with the new Mardi Gras. It is surely no accident that the traditional route for the major Mardi Gras parades (changed in recent years for practical considerations) was down St. Charles Avenue, the principal thoroughfare of the American Garden District, then up and down Canal Street, the dividing line between American uptown and Creole downtown, then into the tight streets of the French Quarter, the snaking parade acting like a thread to bind together the disparate worlds of the city. From its inception Carnival has been this force for social unity and harmony, and it has continued to be such by providing a meeting ground where conflicting attitudes can be acted out and reconciled. This message may be lost on the casual visitor. It may even be missed by most New Orleans residents, at least so far as their conscious awareness of it goes, but surely it is the genius of a great ritual to work on the human mind subliminally and to provide an inner order in the midst of outward pandemonium and frolic.

Notes

1. W. Lloyd Warner, *American Life: Dream and Reality* (Chicago: University of Chicago Press, 1953), pp. 1–26; Ronald L. Grimes, *Symbol and Conquest: Public Ritual and Drama in Santa Fe* (Ithaca and London: Cornell University Press, 1976).

2. Warner, p. 3.

3. Grimes; see especially pp. 21–50, 182–92.

4. Interview of Mrs. D. W., by Glenn A. D'Spain, 1985, from a series of interviews conducted by students of Rosan A. Jordan. We are indebted to Professor Jordan for bringing them to our attention.

5. Errol Hill, *The Trinidad Carnival: Mandate for a National Theatre* (Austin and London: University of Texas Press, 1972), p. 4.

6. Munro S. Edmonson, "Carnival in New Orleans," *Caribbean Quarter* 4 (1956), p. 234.

7. David Elliot Draper, "The Mardi Gras Indians: The Ethnomusicology of Black Americans in New Orleans," Ph.D. dissertation, Tulane University, 1973, p. 8.

8. Ishmael Reed, *Shrovetide in Old New Orleans* (New York: Discus/Avon, 1979), pp. 11–14, 20ff.

9. Phyllis Hutton Raabe, "Status and Its Impact: New Orleans Carnival; the Social Upper Class and Upper Class Power," Ph.D. dissertation, Pennsylvania State University, 1973, p. 181.

10. Ibid., p. 184.

11. Interview of E. C., by Art Callendar, Jr., 1985. Jordan student interview.

12. Edmonson, p. 240.

13. *Ibid.*

14. Interview of R. H. L., by Jan M. Chaisson, 1985. Jordan student interview.

15. Edmonson, p. 242.

16. Raabe, pp. 17–19, 183–85.

17. Edmonson, pp. 240–41.

18. For information on the Mardi Gras Indians, see Draper; Allison Miner, "The Mardi Gras Indians," *Louisiana Folklore Miscellany* 3, no. 3 (1973 for 1972), pp. 48–50; Joan M. Martin, "Mardi Gras Indians, Past and Present," *Louisiana Folklore Miscellany* 3, no. 3 (1973 for 1972), pp. 51–55; and Finn Wilhelmsen, "Creativity in the Songs of the Mardi Gras Indians of New Orleans, Louisiana," *Louisiana Folklore Miscellany* 3, no. 3 (1973 for 1972), pp. 56–74.

19. Robert Tallant, *Mardi Gras* (Garden City: Doubleday, 1948), p. 232. For information on Zulu, see also the New Orleans *Gambit*, 12–18 February 1983; and Lyle Saxon, Edward Dreyer, and Robert Tallant, *Gumbo Ya-Ya: A Collection of Louisiana Folk Tales* (Boston: Houghton Mifflin, 1945), pp. 3–26, which also contains information on the Indians and other Carnival traditions.

20. The phrase "every man a king" passed into Louisiana popular culture with its use in Huey P. Long's gubernatorial campaign of 1927. It eventually became the title of Long's 1933 autobiography. Long took the phrase from William Jennings Bryan and was himself from Protestant north Louisiana, where Mardi Gras is not celebrated, yet it is tempting to see in the phrase at least an echo of the New Orleans penchant for ritual kingship, especially given Long's genius for manipulating every part of the state and the importance of Long in Louisiana's collective consciousness. For discussion of the phrase see T. Harry Williams, *Huey Long: A Biography* (New York: Alfred A. Knopf, 1970), pp. 262, 645.

21. Tallant, p. 107. For the early history of Carnival in New Orleans, see pp. 96–128.

4

Mardi Gras Chase

GLEN PITRE

"There's one! Get him!"

A dozen teenage boys pour from the back of a pick-up truck to dash across a field of sugar cane stubble. Their faces masked, each carries a switch of bamboo or willow or even a cut-down fishing pole, weapons they wave above their heads like sabers as they run.

Their quarry flushes like a rabbit from the brush beside a drainage ditch, a frightened boy who runs with all his heart for the trees that mark the edge of the swamp. The odds are long against him.

A couple of three-wheelers leave the road beside the pick-up. As they roar across the field, their masked riders bounce in their seats as they hit each furrow, closing in on the boy.

But the boy splashes into the swamp before the three-wheelers can flank him. Stumbling on cypress knees as the water grows deeper, he turns to check on his pursuers. He sees them as flashes of gaudy color through the trees, frenzied by the chase and not at all far behind. The boy steps in a hole. Down he goes. He comes up soaked by cold, brown water—and surrounded.

The leader, or "captain," returns order to his masked troop as they escort their captive back to dry ground. There they circle him and make him kneel.

"Say your prayers," instructs the captain. It sounds like a cliché from some late show western, but the prisoner takes it literally.

"Our Father, who art in Heaven, hallowed be thy name . . ."

From *Louisiana Life* 12:1 (1992): 54–60. Reprinted by permission of *Louisiana Life*.

The masked boys begin to tap their sticks against the ground or their pants legs, a rat-tat-tat drone that unnerves the captive.

"Holy Mary, Mother of God, pray for us sinners . . ."

The rat-tat-tat grows louder, rattling the boy. He loses his place, stumbling on the words.

"He doesn't know his prayers," decides the captain. The circle tightens around the boy as the maskers' sticks begin to tap-tap upon his back and arms and legs, measured blows just hard enough to sting. The boy shows off a big, if quivering, grin, weathering his punishment in macho silence. He knows that when he's a year or two older he too can be one of the maskers, wielding a stick of his own, himself teaching the younger boys the price of not knowing their prayers.

So goes Mardi Gras in Choupique, Louisiana, a hamlet along Highway 304 in the swampy backlands north of Thibodaux. Far from being some bizarre aberration, the Shrove Tuesday rituals of Choupique, Vacherie-Gheens, and a few other villages guard the last remnants of Mardi Gras as once practiced all across rural south Louisiana. They maintain a tradition at least as old as the more famous New Orleans carnival or the horseback "Courir de Mardi Gras" of Mamou, Eunice and other prairie towns.

Often told is the story of how in 1755 the Acadians were exiled from Canada and dispersed to the thirteen American colonies, to the West Indies and back to Europe; and how many of those refugees found their way to Louisiana where they started anew, merged with other cultures, and evolved into Cajuns. Less well known is that for many, migration did not end there. By the 1780s Acadians were settling the banks of Bayou Lafourche in southeast Louisiana. But just as their arrival pushed Chawasa and Chitimacha Indians in to the less fertile "back lands," so a generation later did the Sugar Cane Boom push many Cajuns into the backwater swamps as well, giving birth to settlements like Choupique. In their isolated villages they held tightly to the traditions of their forefathers.

When asked how long the Mardi Gras chase had been practiced, Ralph Landry, one of the Choupique maskers, answers, "At least since my Mom and Dad were little.

Probably ever since there was a Choupique." The truth, however, is much longer than that.

According to the medieval European "fête de la quémande," the beggars' feast, certain holidays were set aside when going house to house begging became acceptable behavior. The tradition survives in American culture in forms ranging from trick-or-treat to Christmas caroling. In Louisiana we know it equally well in the parade cry, "Throw me something, Mister!" Certain southwest Louisiana towns practice ritual begging as the "Mardi Gras run" when masked riders go farm to farm on horseback, asking for rice and chasing chickens to make a communal gumbo.

Cultural historians trace Mardi Gras back to the pre-Christian Saturnalia, a Roman fertility festival originally celebrated in December. But according to Professor Barry Ancelet of the Center for Louisiana Studies at USL, many Cajun Mardi Gras traditions derive from the ancient Celts of Scotland, Ireland and Brittany.

"Many Celtic customs, such as use of the whip as a fertility symbol, filtered from Brittany into French Poitou, then came with the Acadians to the New World."

But if Mardi Gras means "Fat Tuesday," a day of revelry, it is also the eve of Lent, a time of abstinence, penitence, and self-denial. In the Middle Ages, sects of "flagellants" made processions through the streets where they beat sin out of onlookers as well.

Whether Mardi Gras whippings originated to encourage fertility or banish sin, in the back lands of Lafourche Parish the tradition continues.

Road maps and English speakers call the town Gheens, but the Cajuns who actually live there say Gheens is only the plantation at the end of the road, a ghost town since a Kentucky candy merchant bought it, mechanized it, sold its mules and evicted its tenants more than a generation ago.

The locals will tell you they live in "la vacherie," "the ranch," a marshy prairie hugging Louisiana 654 east of Bayou Lafourche. The road through town is dead end. One doesn't "pass through" Vacherie-Gheens; one has to be going there. On Mardi Gras day, it's certainly worth the trip.

Festivities begin at noon with a parade, a tradition borrowed from New Orleans a dozen years ago but Cajunized along the way. No closed krewes here. Anyone who shows up with a decorated vehicle and trinkets to throw may participate. Floats range from elaborate home-made affairs to pick-up trucks hastily draped with crepe paper. If half the townsfolk are in the parade, the other half watch from their front yards, diving for beads, with lawn chairs put out for the old folks and blankets spread for the babies.

Lifelong resident Margie Breaux remembers another sort of parade, when as children each year she and others lined the bank of the Company Canal a few days before Mardi Gras to watch the big, colorful floats from New Orleans glide by on barges, en route to be recycled for parades in Houma and Thibodaux. But then as now, even such floating splendor could not compete with the main event, "la course de Mardi Gras," the Mardi Gras chase.

At 2 P.M., after the parade and a hot bowl of gumbo to ward off the chill, teen-age boys and young men gather behind the church. The older veterans, in their late twenties, lay the ground rules and lead the initiation of newcomers. They hand out yard-long willow switches as the boys don their costumes, then make all the first-timers line up against a fence. Each of the other riders files past to strike them a single blow.

"This is so you'll know it can hurt," explains Mark Breaux, Margie's son and the day's unofficial captain. "If we see you whipping people too hard, we'll pay you back for it. Take it easy today. We're not here to hurt anybody."

He begins parceling out tiny round bells that the boys safety-pin to their costumes. As they practice jingling, stories are traded over Mardi Gras past.

"Last year, I didn't even have to catch anybody," one fellow brags through the mouth of his gorilla mask. "When they'd hear my bells, they'd fall down on their knees."

Another boy tops him, "When my pa-pa used to chase, he'd have a hundred bells on his costume. He'd save up all year to buy 'em."

Costumes checked and masks donned, sticks issued and restraint urged, the three dozen riders walk to the trucks where the older men who'll drive them have been waiting hungrily for their chance to be part of the action.

Their caravan files down the single road through town. Horns honk incessantly. The Mardi Gras riders piled in and hanging on yell at whomever they see. Though the trucks aren't yet stopping, small children already fall to their knees, putting their hands together in gestures of supplication.

At the edge of town, riders trade costumes to further conceal their identity and confuse onlookers, then the trucks about face and return more slowly. By now crowds have gathered to await them. At each the caravan stops. Penitents fall to their knees, crying "Pardon! Pardon!" with a French pronunciation, even though in many cases it's the only word of French the children who say it know. Here and there a child cries, but most kids wear the smiles brought by something scary but exciting, roller-coaster smiles.

Men and women, children and adults, seemingly no one is spared a ritual tap-tap. A mother points out her pre-teen son, the knees and elbows of his Sunday best green with grass stains. "Y'all get him good," cries the mother in jest. "He's been bad this year."

When anyone resists, the cry goes up and the chase is on. Once caught, such fighters draw harsher whipping. Fragile bravado must fight back tears, but the captain's watchful eye keeps such rebels from any serious harm.

Occasionally a boy will light out after a girl about his own age, chase her over field and fence, catch her, and carry her back slung over his shoulder. One such "ritual abduction" seems to delight a visiting folklorist as much as it does the participants themselves.

Margie Breaux, whose nine sons each took their turns as chased and chasers, remembers how one of her daughters cried her eyes out one Mardi Gras. A high school majorette at the time, the girl's baton twirling duties had her scheduled for a parade in nearby Lockport Mardi Gras afternoon. She wept the tears of one bereaved that she could not be home to be chased.

As the riders move through town, all sense of organization disappears. Lead trucks creep ahead. Rear trucks fall behind.

Riders drop out to visit, flirt, sample barbecue or simply to enjoy the anonymity their masks and costumes give them. More "riders" join the throng, still in costumes they earlier wore on parade floats. The trucks serve as way stations for the weary under their continually blaring horns.

When the procession reaches the church, everyone switches costumes again to make another pass. Then another. Then another, until everyone is too exhausted to go on.

The day after Mardi Gras, Ash Wednesday, the boy who wore the gorilla mask gets out of school and heads to his job at Burger King. The fellow whose grandfather wore a hundred bells again measures his day by the shipyard whistle. A welder's helper, he tacks together the bulkheads of Coast Guard cutters. And "captain" Mark Breaux once more teaches eighth graders.

There are still people who farm or fish or even trap for a living in Vacherie-Gheens, but many more are carpenters and photographers and computer technicians; a nurse, a dance teacher, and someone studying law. Many fewer people speak French than a generation ago. But anyone too quick to cry over lost traditions should visit here Mardi Gras day.

Perhaps, in one of those ironies of life in the 1990s, the Mardi Gras chase has gone back to serving its ancient pagan purpose: renewal and rebirth. It's not, as in olden times, a plea for fertile crops and fat calves and healthy children. Instead it's a renewal of tradition, a guarantee that notwith-standing fast food, industrial jobs and higher education, the legacies handed down will not be forgotten. Under the tap-tap-tap of the Mardi Gras whips, year after year the old ways will be reborn.

5

The New Orleans King Cake in Southwest Louisiana

MARCIA GAUDET

The feast of the Epiphany, January 6, once marked the close of Advent and the beginning of the Carnival season in many Catholic cultures. On the eve of the Epiphany (Twelfth Night) it was traditional to have a Twelfth Night cake in which a token, usually a bean, was baked. There is evidence of the Twelfth Night cake and bean custom in England, France, Spain, and other parts of Europe as early as the fourteenth century. In New Orleans, Mexico City, and other traditionally French or Spanish Catholic cultures, the Twelfth Night cake custom is still observed.

In New Orleans, Twelfth Night is the beginning of the Mardi Gras season.[1] The New Orleans Twelfth Night Cake or King Cake, as it is usually called today, is a traditional sweet yeast bread served on Twelfth Night and during Mardi Gras season. The New Orleans King Cake is shaped to form a crown, and it is decorated with the traditional Mardi Gras colors using gold, purple, and green sugar. A bean or a small china doll was traditionally baked in the cake, but today a small plastic baby is usually hidden in the cake instead. The person who gets the bean or the baby in a piece of cake is king (or queen) for a week and is expected to provide the next King Cake for the group the following week, and so on

From *Mid-America Folklore* 27 (Fall 1989): 114–21. Reprinted by permission of the author.

until Mardi Gras. The King Cake is available in bakeries throughout the Mardi Gras season, but only during that time. It is served when family and friends gather so the entire cake can be cut and eaten at once.

In an article in the 1965 *Louisiana Folklore Miscellany* on the origin and symbolism of this custom, George Reinecke notes that the Twelfth Night Cake tradition was mainly a New Orleans Creole tradition that was not established in the rural Cajun areas of southwest Louisiana. He also notes that the cakes were usually bought from bakeries, not home baked.[2] In 1970, King Cakes were not available in Lafayette, the hub of the Cajun population, nor was there evidence of home baking. Today the tradition is quite popular in southwest Louisiana, perhaps another example of Cajun-Creole cultural syncretism in Louisiana. This paper will explore the history and symbolism of the tradition of the King Cake and the reasons for the adoption of the New Orleans custom by the people of southwest Louisiana in the past twenty years, a time of increased ethnic pride and cultural awareness for the Cajuns.

The feast of the Epiphany, first celebrated as early as the second century A.D., has been celebrated by the Eastern Orthodox, Roman Catholic and Anglican churches. The Epiphany was traditionally celebrated in Christian countries as the feast of the Magi—the day that the three Wise Men (or "kings") arrived to present gifts to the Christ child—and as the manifestation of Jesus as the Christ. Thus, the finding of the bean or baby is symbolic. The bean or baby (both suggestive of new life) may date earlier to ancient fertility rites, connected with the Saturnalia, since the custom revolves around the choosing of a mock king by chance or lot. As Reinecke suggests, the "fortuitous symbolism" probably led to the Church's encouragement of the ritual.[3] At one time, gift giving, feasting, and bonfires were also celebrated as part of the Epiphany in France and south Louisiana.

The bean cake or king cake celebrations seem to vary widely, both in the form of the cake and the customs surrounding it, but in all forms it involves a king or queen chosen by lot with a token (bean, pecan) in a cake.

Dorothy Spicer describes the tradition in France in the early twentieth century:

> Le Jour des Rois, the Day of the Kings, or Epiphany, is the great festival of childhood in France, as well as in most European and Latin American Countries. Christmas is the season of Holy Birth. But the twelfth day following means a wonderful party with a cake or Kings, games, and laughter. ... Customs and beliefs concerning Three Kings' Day vary widely from place to place. Even the galette des Rois, or cake of the Kings is made differently in the different provinces. But on one point everyone agrees: each cake must contain a bean, a small token, or sometimes a miniature china doll. Usually the galette des Rois is round and flat. It may be honey-spice or sponge inside. It may be decorated with pastry, fruits, or sugared frills.[4]

Spicer says in a 1937 work that in Catholic Germany, a coin or bean was baked in the Epiphany cake, and the Portuguese Epiphany cake had amulets or fortune telling trinkets hidden in it along with one dried lima bean. She also notes that the Mexican rosca de reyes is a crown-shaped cake with a little doll representing the Infant Christ.[5] In a more recent note, Thomas Hale says that at Spring Hill College in Mobile, Alabama, the King Cake has an almond baked in it.[6]

The King Cake custom in Louisiana was of course derived from the French. However, since the custom varied in France, the early customs in Louisiana tended to vary according to the region of France from which the Louisiana French came. The Larousse Gastronomique (1961) says that round flaky pastry is "the symbolic cake eaten on Twelfth Night in most of the provinces north of the Loire," but "in the South, the Twelfth Cake is made of yeast dough in the form of a crown. In both cakes, the symbolic bean is baked in the dough. This is not always, as it used to be, a real bean, but is sometimes a small porcelain model either of a baby emerging from a bean or some other figure."[7] As George Reinecke notes, the New Orleans King Cake is of the southern France tradition of the yeast bread or brioche type, and as such was probably established in its present form by the early nineteenth century French set-tlers who came mainly from Bordeaux and the Pyrenees.[8] Perry Young, however, in *Carnival and Mardi Gras in New Orleans* says the King Cake or Twelfth Night parties were started in New Orleans by the Colonials, and were the first Carnival Balls.[9]

Reinecke's statement that the New Orleans King Cake was traditionally bakery-made and not home baked is supported by my own experience growing up near New Orleans and by an entry in my grandmother's journal, written in 1899, in New Orleans. She writes: "Saturday I went out shopping as usual with my aunt, we came back with a great many small packages . . . my aunt dropped a bag containing a King Cake. Fortunately the bag did not burst so the cake was not spoiled. We ate it at night, one of my cousins getting the pecans." In an earlier entry, she writes: "It being 'King's Day' we ate some King's Cake and my cousins and one of my aunts got the seeds, or as I had better say, the pecans and dolls as two had dolls; my aunt gave me the doll she had."[10] Thus she also supports the idea that the cakes were eaten throughout the Carnival season and that the token varied.

In the Acadian areas of southwest Louisiana, there was a similar custom with a more involved ritual in the late nine-teenth century. The Breaux Manuscript, completed in 1901 by an elderly rural French Louisianian, describes the custom in the Acadian areas as follows:

> Almost all families gather on the eve of this day
> (Kings Day—January 6) at supper to elect by lot the
> "king of the bean"; but it is especially among the
> common folk that the full manner of observing the
> ceremony is preserved.
>
> After supper, a cake is brought out. It is round, and
> encloses a bean. It is cut into as many pieces (plus one)
> as there are members of the family, including the hired
> hands. The pieces are placed in a sack. The youngest
> member of the family withdraws the pieces of the cake;
> he begins by giving the first piece to God. This is given
> to the next poor man who comes to the door and asks
> for help. The second piece goes to the eldest of the family
> and from thence on to the youngest.

The one whose piece contains the bean which had
been placed along one of the edges of the cake is
acclaimed king. All the diners treat him with honor and
must watch him attentively so as not to fail to cry out
"*Le Roi boit*" (the king drinks) whenever he does so.
Failure to conform will result in having the face
besmuttered by the rest of the party.[11]

This description of the Twelfth Night given by a nineteenth century Acadian in Louisiana is very much like that
described by the sixteenth century French writer, Etienne
Pasquier, who points out that the resemblance of the Bean
King to the king of Saturnalia (from the days of imperial
Rome) are striking.[12] Reinecke describes an analogous survival of the custom among the French in Southern Indiana in
his 1965 article.

This tradition among the Cajuns in southwest Louisiana,
however, seems to have been completely gone by the second
half of the twentieth century. Reinecke says that he could find
no evidence of it in southwest Louisiana in the early 1960s,
and when I moved to Lafayette in 1970, the King Cakes were
not available in bakeries in the hub of the Cajun area, nor was
there evidence of home baking. The old Acadian King Cake
Custom is known among some of the older people, but it is no
longer popular or part of the tradition. The cake was referred
to as a *galette*, a thin, flat, biscuit-like cake, much like the King
Cake in the northern provinces of France from which most of
the Acadians originated. A bean was baked in it, and it was
home-baked. Many of the older people in Lafayette and
Crowley said that they did not know this as an older tradition,
but had only heard of it in recent years and described the typical New Orleans King Cake. Thus, there is really nothing genuinely traditional among the Cajuns in the present form of the
King Cake custom in the Cajun region. In its present form it is
imported in imitation of New Orleans.

It is not certain why the custom died out in southwest
Louisiana, but it perhaps had to do with the gradual moving
of other Epiphany customs, such as gift-giving and bonfires, to Christmas as Christmas became a more festive and

important feast. The King Cake custom then became much more associated with Mardi Gras and the beginning of the Carnival season, than with the highlight of the Christmas season, as it had originally been. As Mardi Gras grew in popularity in New Orleans, the King Cake tradition grew along with it. This did not happen among the Cajuns. As the Epiphany was de-emphasized by the Catholic church, the Twelfth Night custom also waned. In addition, there is evidence that the rural Mardi Gras celebrations were not popular in late nineteenth and early twentieth century with the Acadians. The Breaux Manuscript notes that in the late nineteenth century "In the rural areas, carnival has lost its former animation; it is marked nowadays [1901] only by some unimaginative masquerading and by dances where the joyous madness of yesteryear is rarely to be met."[13] (This is no longer true, with the return of the *Courir de Mardi Gras* among the Cajuns.)

However, the fact is that the King Cake tradition was not maintained in the Cajun areas, while it grew in popularity in New Orleans. Sometime during the mid-seventies the King Cake custom began to gain popularity in southwest Louisiana. Today, the tradition is quite popular in the Acadian areas of southern Louisiana, perhaps due to commercialization by the *boulangeries* (bakeries), and there is a trend toward home baking. However, the King Cake currently popular in southwest Louisiana is not the *galette des rois* of the Cajuns, but the New Orleans yeast-type brioche King Cake, complete with the decorative sugars tinted gold, purple, and green, the traditional colors of Mardi Gras.

These "traditional" colors, gold, purple, and green, are from the flag of the Krewe of Rex, King of New Orleans Mardi Gras. The flag was designed in 1872, and since then the colors have been closely associated with Mardi Gras. Reinecke does not mention the colored sugars as being gold, purple, and green in his 1965 article (just "colored sugars to represent jewels") and the use of these colors on the cakes is probably a relatively recent tradition. In the 1971 book *American Cooking: Creole and Acadian*, however, Peter S. Feibleman says: "Traditionally the cake is decorated with sugar tinted in the classic carnival colors: green, purple, and yellow."[14]

The current popularity of the King Cake is apparent both in New Orleans and southwest Louisiana. Grocery stores and bakeries throughout Acadiana advertise the King Cakes, and recipes are beginning to appear in newspapers and cookbooks. There is a King Cake Mix, a brioche-type yeast cake complete with colored sugars and a plastic baby, available in grocery stores, and New Orleans based Popeye's Fried Chicken in Lafayette gives a free King Cake with a family size order of fried chicken during the Carnival season. Special orders are also popular. For example, Poupart's Bakery in Lafayette has baked a King Cake for 200 for a party.

Poupart's Bakery also advertises both an "American" and a "French" King Cake. They refer to the New Orleans King Cake with the colored sugars as the "American King Cake" and the northern France flaky pastry as the "French King Cake." The "French" cake is a round and flat flaky pastry. It has a token in it, and a gold paper crown on top. The "French" cake is much more like the old Cajun *galette des rois* than the more popular King Cake. The Pouparts, who are from Paris, opened their bakery in Lafayette in 1969, and their "French" king cake is the traditional northern France King Cake.

Keller's Bakery, the oldest bakery in Lafayette (1929), bakes a slightly different King Cake. It has a white icing and candy beads decorating it, but no colored sugars. It has the baby hidden in it, and it is a filled cake with a caramel and nut filling. Like the others, it is baked only during Carnival season. This may indicate actually the older New Orleans tradition. The Kellers (now retired) were originally from New Orleans. Their daughter and son now run the bakery, and they said they use their father's old recipe from New Orleans for their King Cakes. They did not make them when they first opened the bakery, because there was no demand for them. They began to make them in Lafayette about fifteen years ago.

It is interesting to note that the King Cake custom is also still popular in France. A graduate student at the University of Southwestern Louisiana from northern France says that they are still very popular in northern France throughout carnival season. They are not decorated with colored sugars, but both a pastry type cake and the brioche cake are used. The cakes are almost all bakery-made in France also. Sometimes a china doll is in the cake and sometimes other trinkets or good luck charms such as horseshoes or four leaf clovers are put into the cakes instead. This is analogous to the New Orleans area custom of putting similar trinkets (ring, thimble, button, heart, horseshoe, etc.) into the wedding cake, attached to ribbons to be "pulled" by the unmarried women friends of the bride.

The current growing popularity of the King Cakes in southwest Louisiana seems to be another example of Cajun-Creole cultural syncretism in Louisiana. Though the diverse origins of the Cajuns, Creoles, and nineteenth century French immigrants to Louisiana are clear, the customs and traditions of each group and particularly the foodways, have often been accepted and adopted by the other in south Louisiana. The feeling seems to be that if it is French, it must be part of my heritage too. Though Cajuns certainly have a vast and rich store of cultural traditions and foodways, they seemed always willing to borrow and adapt. (For example, the accordian, introduced by the Germans in Louisiana in the nineteenth century is now considered an essential part of Cajun music. In foodways, spicy seasonings are from the Spanish, filé from the Indians, and okra from Africans or Black Creoles.)

In an area and ethnic culture with widely recognized ethnic foodways, the Cajun and Creole cuisine, the King Cake is a festive, special occasion cake. It seems to be bought and eaten primarily to participate in the tradition, even when in some cases it is a rather dry coffee roll. Cajuns in general identify very strongly with their traditional foodways, particularly things like crawfish, boudin and gumbo. The King Cake, however, does not seem to function in this way. It does not seem to be a symbol of ethnic identity for them as much as it is a means or way to participate in the carnival season without requiring masking or becoming involved with carnival krewes or attending parades, etc. The form of the cake is not crucial, since it is acceptable in several forms, and there is little or no importance to the preparation since the cakes are traditionally bakery-made or store bought. What is important is participating in some way in a festive occasion, the Mardi Gras season, which does have a strong cultural tradition in south Louisiana and one no longer closely tied to one ethnic group (except for the running Mardi Gras of the rural Cajuns). In a sense, it transcends their "Cajunicity," if you will, and makes them a part of the larger cultural concept of French-American South Louisiana. Finding the token in the cake and cutting and sharing the cake with friends are the important things. Though the Mardi Gras season has always been important culturally in New Orleans, it is growing more important in the Acadian area with both the Carnival balls in the larger towns and cities and the rural *courir de Mardi Gras*. Though the King Cake in its present form is imported in imitation of the New Orleans tradition, it is a French tradition with a past history in Acadiana. While it is certain that some of the popularity is due to commercialization by the bakeries and the influence of transplanted New Orleanians, the custom in its new form seems to be more than a fad. It is true that its popularity is centered mainly in the more urban areas of Acadiana, but its popularity is growing. It also provides both Cajuns and "newcomers" a means of participating in a food custom that is certainly easier to adapt to than eating boudin and crawfish.

While the present form of the cake is not genuinely traditional with the southwest Louisiana Cajuns, the celebration of Mardi Gras and the Carnival season is. Thus, it is a symbolic link with a tradition of long standing. It is a regional, cultural, festive food custom that originated as a religious folk way (Epiphany) and became a festival cake associated with Mardi Gras. In spite of the fact that it does have some marks of a seasonal "fad," the ritual surrounding the King Cake is important, though in a much simpler form. A group of family or friends gather, the cake is cut and eaten, someone gets the "baby" and gets to be King or Queen, with only the obligation of providing the next King Cake. Even this is not an absolute rule and only applies when a group agrees that this is what will be done.

The King Cake is a symbolic food that together with the ritual of finding the "baby" provides an enjoyable way to participate in the culture. Barre Toelken points out that the symbolic foods and rituals of Thanksgiving serve as symbols of unity, with others and with the past.[15] The King Cake has a similar function. Rather than a symbol of ethnic identity, the King Cake seems to be a symbol of participation in cultural festivities with which the participants identify.

Much has been written on the importance of ethnic food-ways as symbols of identity. Janet Theophano, in writing about Greek festival foods, sees festival and holiday food as especially important in creating bonds between members of a group, both past and present.[16] With a food custom so closely associated with a cultural festival or tradition with which one has strong ties, this function of symbol and iden-tity works even if the form of the food itself is not genuinely traditional, such as the case of the New Orleans King Cake in the Acadiana area of southwest Louisiana, and even if the cul-tural group with which one is identifying includes more than one's own more limited ethnic group identity as a Cajun. The New Orleans King Cake among the Cajuns symbolically ties them with the New Orleans-based non-Cajun French culture in Louisiana. In addition, it perhaps shows a reciprocal side of the relatively new found acceptance of the Cajuns and the Cajun culture by people in the New Orleans area, who now, rather than denigrating the Cajuns, are emphasizing their cultural links and shared French heritage.

Notes

1. Traditionally, the eve of the Epiphany is called Twelfth Night and the Epiphany (January 6) is Twelfth Day. In Louisiana today, January 6 is typically celebrated as Twelfth Night.

2. George J. Reinecke, "The New Orleans Twelfth Night Cake," *Louisiana Folklore Miscellany* 2:1 (April 1965), pp. 45–47.

3. Reinecke, p. 52.

4. Dorothy Gladys Spicer, *Feast Day Cakes from Many Lands* (New York: Holt, Rinehart, and Winston, 1960), p. 17.

5. Dorothy Gladys Spicer, *The Book of Festivals* (The Woman's Press, 1937), pp. 132, 225, 266.

6. Thomas Hale, "The Kings' Cake Custom in Mobile, Alabama," *Louisiana Folklore Miscellany* 2:4 (August 1968), p. 104.

7. Reinecke, pp. 45–46, quoting from Prosper Montagne, *Larousse Gastronomique* (New York: Crown, 1961).

8. Reinecke, p. 47.

9. Perry Young, *Carnival and Mardi Gras in New Orleans* (New Orleans: Harmanson, 1939), p. 10.

10. Unpublished Journal of Alice Berthelot Gendron, New Orleans, Louisiana, 1899.

11. Anonymous Breaux Manuscript, "Early Louisiana French Life and Folklore," ed. Jay K. Ditchy, trans. George F. Reinecke, *Louisiana Folklore Miscellany* 2:3 (May 1966), pp. 29–30.

12. Clement A. Miles, *Christmas Customs and Traditions: Their History and Significance* (New York: Dover Publications, 1976), pp. 339–40.

13. Breaux Manuscript, p. 21.

14. Peter S. Feibleman, ed., *American Cookery: Creole and Acadian* (New York: Time-Life Books, 1971), p. 62.

15. Barre Toelken, *The Dynamics of Folklore* (Boston: Houghton-Mifflin, 1979), pp. 131–36.

16. Janet Theophano, "Feast, Fast and Time," *Pennsylvania Folklife* (Spring 1978), p. 25.

6

Christmas Bonfires in South Louisiana

Tradition and Innovation

MARCIA GAUDET

Christmas season bonfires, once popular in France, Germany, other parts of Europe, and the British Isles, continue to be part of the Christmas celebration in a small area along the Mississippi River in south Louisiana. After dark on Christmas Eve, huge bonfires blaze along the levees of the river in the parishes of St. James, St. John the Baptist, and Ascension. (This area includes about 30 miles of levee on each side of the river and is located about midway between New Orleans and Baton Rouge.) These bonfires, built of logs, cane reed, and bamboo, create the effect of spectacular fireworks. Large crowds of family, friends, and visitors gather on the levee to watch the bonfires, sometimes built as close as 20 to a mile of levee. A popular explanation for the bonfires is "to light the way for Papa Noel."

Though this holiday custom is now practiced by people of Acadian French and German descent, it was probably not a custom practiced by the original Acadian and German settlers but reintroduced by the nineteenth century French immigrants. This could explain why the custom is not observed by the Cajuns on the bayous or the prairies of southwest Louisiana or, in general, by people on the First German Coast (St. Charles Parish). The custom was probably established in St. James Parish between 1880 and 1900. Father Louis Poche, a Jesuit priest and native of St. James Parish, remembers hearing

From *Southern Folklore* 47:3 (1990): 195–206. Reprinted by permission of University Press of Kentucky.

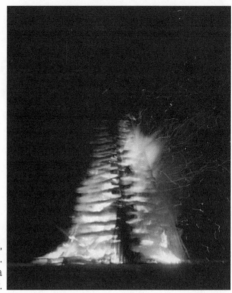

Christmas bonfire,
Vacherie, 1995.
Photo by Marcia
Gaudet.

from his family that the bonfire custom in Louisiana was started in St. James by the French Marist priests who came to Louisiana after the Civil War to teach at Jefferson College, then a Catholic college in Convent, Louisiana (1979). In a recent oral history project on bonfires, the German-Acadian Coast Historical and Genealogical Society found oral documentation that a former Jefferson College student, George Bourgeois, began building bonfires in Mt. Airy (near Gramercy) in 1884 and that he had known the custom as a student of the Marist priests (Guidry 1990). Alcée Fortier, however, does not mention bonfires in his descriptions of holiday customs in his 1894 *Louisiana Studies*, though he was born and raised in St. James Parish and graduated from Jefferson College. A note in *Louisiana History* dates the bonfires from about 1897 but does not give the source of this date ("Louisiana Christmas" 1972). In *Cabanocey*, Lillian Bourgeois describes the bonfire tradition in St. James Parish in Louisiana and says that they originated near Convent on New Year's Eve and were built on the *batture*. In the 1950s, she says, they were moved to the levee and lit on Christmas Eve (1957: 154). My own childhood memories of bonfires in St. John the Baptist Parish in the 1940s and 1950s are that they were very much an established Christmas tradition but much smaller and built in one or two days.

While lighting bonfires as part of ritual and celebration is ancient in origin, the continuing fascination with bonfires and fireworks as part of religious ritual, community celebration, and tourist spectacle has been noted. Stanley Brandes discusses the religious and secular elements of fireworks in the *Fiesta de Febrero* in Tzintzuntzan (1981), and Venetia Newall discusses the relation of the social setting to two English fire festivals (1972). Vladimir Propp says in a study of Russian festivals that prior to the nineteenth century at Christmas time "big bonfires were made, and the dead were called to warm themselves" (1987: 236). Regina Bendix notes that in 1805, in Interlaken, Madame de Staël was "particularly taken with the bonfires lit on the surrounding hilltops that commemorated the fires of liberty of the original Swiss confederation" (1989: 131).

The French expression for bonfire is *feu de joie,* or "fire of joy." In *Manuel de folklore Français contemporain,* Arnold Van Gennep explains the custom of the *feux de joie* in France and says that the *feux de joie* were part of religious holiday celebrations and were held several times a year, including the Eve of the Epiphany, New Year's Eve, Christmas Eve, and in some places the feast of the patron saint. In other parts of France they were held only on the Eve of the Epiphany or on Christmas Eve. Much of this custom in France disappeared in the early twentieth century (Van Gennep 1958: 3033–3068). The holiday bonfire custom in south Louisiana seems to have definitely been derived from the French custom. In *Tales from the Levee,* I attempt to trace the origins of the bonfires in this area and describe them at that time as "a true folk tradition" that has "escaped, so far, any involvement with commercialism," though there were some indications of change and variations in the shapes of the pyres (Gaudet 1984: 9–14). Nicholas Spitzer refers to the *feux de joie* and the rural Mardi Gras as "traditional folk events" in Louisiana (1985: 78).

Until the past few years, lighting bonfires on the levee on Christmas Eve was a true folk tradition in this area. Like many folk customs that come to the attention of the media and tourists, however, the bonfires seem to have changed considerably, becoming a spectacle with questionable tradition and shades of pyromania, along with ordinances to regulate them, complaints from ecologists, and commercialism. In the last five years, there have been definite changes in the bonfires, with major media coverage from the television stations in Baton Rouge and New Orleans and reporters from as far away as Atlanta. They have become a spectacular pyrotechnic display, drawing over 40,000 visitors in the last few years.

The traditional shape of the bonfires is that of a tepee though there have been some variations, such as the square pyre (or "fort"), and beginning in 1975, small log cabins and ships. The construction of the bonfire pyres usually begins shortly after Thanksgiving. Traditionally the young boys and young men get together to cut and gather logs along the river or in the swampy woods behind their homes, and each bonfire is planned and built by an informal group of family and friends. Usually there is a recognized "leader" of each bonfire, though this is an informal designation, who lights the fire on Christmas Eve. There is no definite time to light the fire other than "when it gets dark." Though individuals buy and use fireworks at the bonfires, there is no organized or central fireworks display. There is also no use of costumes or disguises, no begging or mumming, and no procession of participants, though now there is a motor procession of spectators, mainly from Baton Rouge and New Orleans, who drive their cars along the River Road. Drinking is a usual part of the celebration, but food is typically a part of the later get-together in the homes.

Along with the more traditional bonfires, since 1985 there have been spectacular pyres built in the shape of symbols of wealth and power. In 1985 one bonfire pyre was in the shape of a local antebellum mansion with two circular staircases and even an outhouse. The pyre was so large and well constructed that people could walk up to the second floor and the widow's walk on the roof. Other spectacular pyres have been a replica of the Louisiana Superdome (1987), an offshore oil rig platform (1987), and a train with four cars (1988). These bonfires are no longer mainly built by the young people but often by organized groups. For example, the Gramercy Fire Department builds a

Building a bonfire on the levee in Gramercy, December 24, 1999. Photo by Marcia Gaudet.

novelty bonfire each year and sells gumbo, beer, and souvenirs as a fund raiser. The atmosphere at these bonfires is somewhat like Carnival in New Orleans, along with cotton candy vendors and souvenir "bonfires" for sale. Indications of the importance of the bonfires in this part of Louisiana are the "bonfire aprons" given to customers by a local bank, a pen and ink sketch of a bonfire pyre by an artist with prints for sale, and several "bonfire" Christmas cards. Zapp's Potato Chips in Gramercy has a special Christmas package with a drawing of a bonfire and "Gramercy—Christmas Bonfire Capital of the World" written under it. All of these feature the traditional tepee shaped bonfire pyre.

There have been innovations in the shapes of the pyres since 1975 (small log cabin), and some of these changes are certainly because of the long standing tradition in the area of trying to build the biggest and best bonfire. The building of spectacular pyres, however, is surely encouraged by the media attention and tourists. The media coverage began in the mid

Bonfire pyre, 1985. Photo by Gene Chabaud.

1970s and has increased each year along with the crowds of visitors.

The builders of the bonfires, however, do not feel that they are built for tourism. The river parishes are not a major tourist area, other than for tours of antebellum homes, and tourism does not have a large economic impact on the area. There are few motels or restaurants. Nolan Oubre, Fire Chief of the Gramercy Volunteer Fire Department, noted that even the novelty or "tourist" bonfires are "not primarily to attract tourists or to make money" but are a matter of tradition and community pride. He explained that the Gramercy Fire Department started serving gumbo and providing portable toilets as a convenience for visitors since there are few restaurants or restrooms available along the River Road. He also pointed out that most visitors return to New Orleans or Baton Rouge after viewing the bonfires (1989).[1]

It is interesting that changes in the bonfires and the building of pyres that symbolize wealth and power coincide with a time of severe economic depression in Louisiana, beginning in 1985. Perhaps the increased novelty of the pyres heightens the celebration and lifts the spirits, in addition to providing fund-raising opportunities for community groups. Other holiday customs in this area (e.g. the King's cake and Mardi Gras) do not seem to have changed noticeably in recent years except that, like the bonfires, they are less family centered. The focus on the bonfires in this area and the resulting pride is perhaps due to the common belief that it is a unique Christmas custom.

Until the late 1970s there was no regulation of the bonfires. With increased media coverage there were also many complaints by environmentalists and ecologists, and some of the area governments approved ordinances to regulate the bonfires and restrict their size. Much of the real "hype" came after these attempts at control.

According to Fire Chief Nolan Oubre, all bonfires must have permits from the Levee Board. Since Gramercy is an incorporated town, rules must be submitted to the Levee Board for approval. The following are Levee Board regulations, as specified by Fire Chief Oubre:

1. Fires must be at least 125 feet apart.
2. Fires can be no higher than 25 feet. (This rule went into effect in 1987; it was 28 feet for a few years prior to 1987; before then, there were no regulations.)
3. Fires can be no larger than the crown of the levee— 12 feet in diameter.
4. No tires, creosote, or "foreign matter" may be used, due to environmental concerns.
5. Each town is allowed one "tourist attraction" with no regulations at all.

In Gramercy, the Volunteer Fire Department has the "tourist" bonfire. In 1987, the media estimated that over 40,000 people visited the Gramercy fires. The Volunteer Fire Department served over 20,000 plates of gumbo for the event, which supports the department. On the east bank of St. James Parish, there were 97 fires in 1987. The fire chief in each town determines if the fires can be lit on Christmas Eve, based on the wind factor. Clean-up must be done the morning after because of the Levee Board's insistence, and the townspeople of Gramercy perform this task because of their community pride in the event (Oubre 1988).

The building of the fires, in addition, has become a kind of folk craft. Building a good bonfire, i.e., one that will burn evenly without collapsing prematurely, requires skill. The designing and building skills have been demonstrated at folk craft festivals in other parts of Louisiana.

Several things are occurring at once in the bonfire tradition. The obvious reaction to tourism and media has resulted in commercialism. On the other hand, the reaction to attempted restrictions and regulations has resulted in more people getting involved in the activity. Though the "spectacle" type bonfires draw the crowds, the more traditional bonfires continue more or less unchanged, except for the traffic congestion on the River Road. We see here both a holiday custom being maintained in the traditional way, with the traditional meanings, and a show being put on for spectators, for fund raising, for publicity, for the "fun of it," i.e., to have a good time. This duality is possible because of the dynamics of the custom. The bonfires once were basically a private holiday celebration of small groups of family and friends gathering to celebrate Christmas with a bonfire, much like a private birthday celebration. There was no community organization or planning. The nature of the private celebration, of course, made it highly visible to the public since the bonfires were built on the top of the levees of the river, and the spectacle of all these fires burning and reflecting in the river drew the attention of the media.

There is, of course, the question of traditionality. Can the bonfires still be called traditional or folk custom? What is it that makes them traditional? Certainly celebrating Christmas by lighting a bonfire is traditional in this area—like the lighting of the Yule log and the lighting of the candles on a birthday cake. The bonfire builders seem to be aware of tradition in building the fires or at least a sense of continuing something that has been done before. The event is also something that is genuinely enjoyed by all the people and regarded as a "good time" by the young. As Venetia Newall notes with two English fire festivals, this fun factor is also a vital part of the survival of the bonfires (1972: 245).

It is not really the shape per se of the bonfires that changed the nature of the celebrations because for the past 12 years different shapes have been utilized. Of more importance is the nature of the group involved. Traditionally, and still the case for the majority of bonfires, a close-knit crowd of mainly family and friends celebrates together what is basically a private occasion in a highly visible space. The event is quite a different matter when the crowd is so large that they neither know each other nor the builders of the fire and when gumbo and drinks are sold to visitors.

The changes in the bonfire celebration reflect, among other things, the changing attitudes toward Christmas and how it should be celebrated. For some it is no longer a private or family-centered Christmas celebration but is a secular festival to entertain "outsiders" and attract media coverage. The bonfires have been compared, in fact, to a "one-day Mardi Gras" or Carnival season. While the builders of the more spectacular bonfires make this comparison with pride, this aspect is disturbing to other more traditionally inclined people in the area who feel that this kind of Carnival atmosphere is inappropriate on Christmas Eve. In discussing a similar attitude toward Christmas and Carnival on Saint Vincent, Roger Abrahams points out that Christmas is "a time of restraint when one reaffirms one's place in the community, while Carnival is a time when one loses one's identity through masking and other licentious activities." Abrahams further observes that "Carnival is properly played on the street, while Christmas performances are given in the yard; this is a physical differentiation of great symbolic importance to the Vincentian, for as noted the yard is the family place, the place of privacy, while the street is almost synonymous with sportiness, rudeness, dissension and trouble" (1972: 278).

Something quite similar is operating in the bonfire situation because in many ways the levee is an extension of the yard for the property owners along the river. The levee is much more like the sidewalk through one's property than a street since the property owners do own the *batture* between the levee and the river and they maintain certain traditional rights to the levee, such as being able to fence it in or build a gazebo on it—though few people do this anymore. The communities are built along the river, and those who have property on the River Road are likely to host bonfires or, in the case of older residents, to give permission to people they know or to an organized group to build a bonfire in front of their property. According to Fire Chief Oubre, though the levee is owned by the State of Louisiana and the landowners actually have no control over what goes on, there are some rights that have been traditionally observed. Some landowners do object and do not want a bonfire in front of their homes, and the town observes this courtesy. Many feel that the bonfires become too much like a Carnival, with the problems of traffic, noise, and general littering which leaves the levee in a mess on Christmas morning, and they prefer the smaller, more traditional bonfires.

The bonfires are in a time of peak transition; they are still linked with the religious holiday (Christmas Eve) but with no overtly religious dimensions. Like most traditional celebrations, the term *festival* is not applied by local people to the bonfire celebrations (See Stoeltje 1983: 239). However, the tourist bonfires certainly have the aspects of a festival presented as a spectacle for outside consumption and featuring "rites of conspicuous display" (Mesnil 1976: 24–27; Falassi 1987: 4). Though it is generally accepted by scholars that customs and traditions change and are even invented (Hobsbawm and Ranger 1983; Ben-Amos 1984; Handler and Linnekin 1984; Bendix 1989), the tourist bonfires seem to cause some conflict within the culture group since some members of the community see the festival-like celebration as inappropriate for Christmas. With the spectacle of the fires and the fascination with the craft of the "tourist pyres," however, this aspect of the bonfires is becoming an established and generally accepted part of the holiday custom.

An interesting aspect of the bonfires is the growing sense of "tradition" from the perspective of visitors. According to several New Orleans natives, the Christmas Eve ritual for many New Orleans families has become the car trip "up the River Road" to see the bonfires, either in the afternoon to see the "tourist" pyres or at night to see other fires.[2] There are also bonfire boat tours on the river.

Though the "spectacle" type bonfires draw the crowds and media coverage, the smaller, less elaborate, more traditional bonfires continue off the main path of the spectators and are still very much part of a folk tradition. We see, therefore, both a custom being maintained in the traditional way and a show being put on for spectators. Because of the nature of this holiday custom, essentially an individual or private tradition, but a highly visible individual observance, it is possible for the folk tradition to be maintained while at the same time and in the same area, it has become a spectacle for visitors and media.

Notes

1. My sister Gayle Hymel, a resident of St. James Parish, arranged for me to interview Fire Chief Oubre and directed me to other aspects of the contemporary bonfires.
2. Folklorist Sean Galvin, whose family lives in New Orleans, called this tradition to my attention (personal communication 1988).

References

Abrahams, Roger D. 1972. Christmas and Carnival on Saint Vincent. *Western Folklore* 31: 275–89.

Ben-Amos, Dan. 1984. The Seven Strands of Tradition: Varieties in Its Meaning in American Folklore Studies. *Journal of Folklore Research* 21: 97–131.

Bendix, Regina. 1989. Tourism and Cultural Displays: Inventing Traditions for Whom? *Journal of American Folklore* 102: 131–46.

Bourgeois, Lillian. 1957. *Cabanocey: The History, Customs and Folklore of St. James Parish.* New Orleans: Pelican Publishing.

Brandes, Stanley H. 1981. Fireworks and Fiestas: The Case from Tzintzuntzan. *Journal of Latin American Lore* 7: 171–90.

Falassi, Alessandro. 1987. Festival Definition and Morphology. In *Time Out of Time: Essays on the Festival*, ed. Alessandro Falassi, 1–10. Albuquerque: University of New Mexico Press.

Fortier, Alcée. 1894. *Louisiana Studies.* New Orleans: F. F. Hansell.

Gaudet, Marcia. 1984. *Tales from the Levee: The Folklore of St. John the Baptist Parish.* Lafayette: Center for Louisiana Studies.

Guidry, Emily. 1990. Telephone interview, 4 January.

Handler, Richard, and Jocelyn Linnekin. 1984. Tradition, Genuine or Spurious. *Journal of American Folklore* 97: 273–90.

Hobsbawm, Eric, and Terence Ranger, eds. 1983. *The Invention of Tradition.* Cambridge: Cambridge University Press.

Louisiana Christmas on Mississippi River Levee. 1972. *Louisiana History* 8: 368–70.

Mesnil, Marianne. 1976. The Masked Festival: Disguise or Affirmation? *Culture* 3: 11–29.

Newall, Venetia J. 1972. Two English Fire Festivals in Relation to Their Contemporary Social Setting. *Western Folklore* 31: 244–74.

Oubre, Nolan. 1988. Telephone interview, 10 October.

————. 1989. Interview with author. Gramercy, Louisiana, 24 December.

Poche, Reverend Louis. 1979. Interview with author. Grand Coteau, Louisiana, 8 June.

Propp, Vladimir. 1987. The Commemoration of the Dead. In *Time Out of Time: Essays on the Festival*, ed. Alessandro Falassi, 231–43. Albuquerque: University of New Mexico Press.

Spitzer, Nicholas R., ed. 1985. *Louisiana Folklife: A Guide to the State*. Baton Rouge: Louisiana Folklife Program.

Stoeltje, Beverly J. 1983. Festival in America. In *Handbook of American Folklore*, ed. Richard M. Dorson, 239–46. Bloomington: Indiana University Press.

Van Gennep, Arnold. 1958. *Manuel de folklore Français contemporain*. Vol. 7. Paris: A. et J. Picard et Cie.

7

The Creole Tradition

Michael Tisserand

"Le plus ça change, le plus ça reste pareil."
The more things change the more they stay the same . . .

It was long past midnight in late 1965 when a station wagon, filled with laughing men, barreled down the narrow Railroad Avenue in Welsh, Louisiana. When Creole fiddler Canray Fontenot heard the commotion, he got out of bed and pulled his clothes on. "I knew there was something serious somewhere," he remembers.

Indeed there was. Fontenot watched as the car rolled to a stop in his driveway and his longtime musical partner, accordionist Alphonse "Bois-Sec" Ardoin, stepped out, followed by a man Fontenot didn't recognize: Ralph Rinzler, a trained folklorist who had come to Louisiana looking for performers for the 1966 Newport Folk Festival in Rhode Island.

The party moved inside, and the musicians set up their instruments for an informal late night audition. Fontenot looked into Rinzler's eager face, and he couldn't help but recall a conversation he'd had not too long before with another friend, Clifton Chenier, by then a well-traveled zydeco bandleader.

"Where are you working tonight?" Chenier had asked.

"I ain't working nowhere," replied the fiddler. "Man, it's eight years now I don't play. I done sold my stuff."

Chenier wouldn't hear of this. "Aw man, you quit at the wrong time! You can't do that!"

"I done done it," replied Fontenot matter-of-factly.

From *Louisiana Cultural Vistas* (Fall 1994): 20–29. Reprinted by permission of the author.

"No man, tell you what. You're the best Negro on the fiddle here in Louisiana, and I'm the best on the accordion. Things is just beginning to get good."

"Wha—?"

"Aw man, that music is going to move up North," Chenier insisted. "Go get you a fiddle and start playing, and the first thing you know they're going to want you all over the world."

So, as Fontenot tells the story, it was thanks to Clifton Chenier's urging that, when Rinzler showed up at his house in 1965, he still had one fiddle left unsold, an instrument that a trash truck driver had salvaged for him, a "bad luck" fiddle that had been tossed out when its player fell ill and died.

After a few songs were played, Rinzler invited Ardoin and Fontenot to Rhode Island for the following July, for the performance which would introduce Creole music to its widest audience yet. "Boy was I embarrassed with this little fiddle here," recalls Fontenot. "But I said, 'Lord have mercy, what the hell'—I had never went to a festival before."

Never full-time musicians, 80-year-old Ardoin and 74-year-old Fontenot have put their instruments up on blocks many times during their lives. Their rhythmic, bluesy playing and ancient melodies have not always been in fashion— "I had to put my accordion on the armoire because they all wanted rock and roll," recalls Ardoin of one dry spell. And both men always had other things on their minds besides music: Ardoin raised 14 children by working as a farmer, Fontenot his six by laboring in a Welsh seed store.

But each time they return to their instruments–and fans from Newport to New Iberia have not let them rest long in the most recent decades—the rural Creole culture of southern Louisiana regains one of its earliest and most vibrant voices. What they play is not the more rhythm-and-blues influenced zydeco, Ardoin and Fontenot will repeatedly tell you, nor is it Cajun.

No, they say, call the music what you call its players: Creole.

The Creole Tradition: Two Men

From the Spanish *criolla*, meaning native to the locality, the definition of "Creole" changes as you move throughout Louisiana. Black Creole music in the southern region reflects a complex historical mingling of people, including enslaved Africans, European colonists, Cajuns, Haitian "gens libres de couleur," and Native American tribes.

But there's probably a simpler way to describe Creole music: it's whatever Canray Fontenot and Bois-Sec Ardoin choose to play. In their practiced hands, a European dance form like the waltz is reinvented into a bluesy tune like "Bonsoir Moreau," infiltrated with polyrhythms that bespeak African and African-Caribbean influences.

In concert, when Fontenot and Ardoin reach a midpoint in their song, they shoot each other knowledgeable glances, release slight smiles and bear down on their instruments, tap their feet harder, go to work, drive a deeper groove down the median of the tune. That's Creole music.

During an afternoon conversation at his home in Welsh, Fontenot speaks much the same way as he improvises on a song, pulling on his vowels like blue notes, drawing out an extended "we-e-e-ll . . ." before launching into another story. The fiddler's clear memories of a Louisiana childhood reveal the roots of Creole life, music and culture to be entwined at the deepest levels.

Fontenot has recorded many of the festive seasonal songs he loved to listen to when he was a child in the community of L'Anse aux Vaches. He remembers that at Christmas, "My grandpa would get a bunch of men together and sing all night there . . . a little log was put in the chimney, and they'd let it burn all night long. Before sunup Christmas morning, everybody would take twelve coals out of the Christmas fire to make the calendar in the barn. Then they would take some onion, some salt garlic, and believe me, they could tell you if this month was going to be a wet month, if there was going to be a lot of rain."

By this time, young Canray had already decided he was going to join the ranks of his family's musicians. His father,

Adam Fontenot, was one of the most popular accordionists in the area, but Fontenot was even more intrigued by a cousin named Douglas Belair, who played fiddle and is credited as the first black Creole to record. After separating from his wife, Belair moved to Fontenot's neighborhood, where he soon grew accustomed to seeing nine-year-old Canray at his door.

"I used to go fool with the fiddle, you know, I had learned how to tune it and everything from him," remembers Fontenot. "But he started getting kind of popular and most of the time that doggone Douglas was gone. I didn't have nothing to practice—how in the hell was I going to learn? I was just getting in the groove to learn something, now he keeps taking the fiddle."

The solution took the shape of a wooden cigar box, some screen taken from an unsuspecting mother's new door, some sewing thread, pine-tree rosin and a knife spirited away from a drunken meat cutter. "It didn't sound loud, but I could hear what I was doing," says Fontenot, adding that he repeated the construction once, for a museum somewhere in France.

Bois-Sec Ardoin grew up in the community of L'Anse de 'Prien Noir, where his father died when he was only two. He remembers house dances on weekends during his childhood, and he once found a guitar in the attic. He asked his mother if it belonged to his father. She told him he had never played anything.

Hard work was the constant for the Ardoin brothers as they helped their mother sharecrop. But, during a Sunday afternoon conversation with his son, Morris, Bois-Sec also turns the talk to his dubious reputation for avoiding labor. Born Alphonse Ardoin, Bois-Sec is almost universally addressed by his nickname, which translates to "Dry-Wood." He acquired the moniker at an early age, when he was helping in the fields as a water boy. When it would rain, the older men would wait it out in the field, while Bois-Sec made a dash to the barn.

When these stories begin this afternoon, Morris Ardoin is seized with what soon becomes nearly uncontrollable laughter. "He was raised not to stand in the rain," he manages to get out. His father stares straight ahead, a smile beginning to trace across his face, as Morris recalls stories of Bois-Sec falling asleep in the morning dew, sometimes on ant hills.

Alphonse "Bois-Sec" Ardoin, in his family graveyard near his home. 1994. Photo by Marcia Gaudet.

Bois-Sec first started playing music on his brother's accordion, which he'd take to the top of the barn to avoid getting caught. His brother eventually discovered him and gave him the instrument. But the way Bois-Sec Ardoin played and sang would be changed forever when he heard the voice of his cousin, Amede Ardoin.

The Legacy of Amede Ardoin

A distinctive accordion player, an emotional singer and a legendary songwriter, Amede Ardoin is one of the most important progenitors of both Cajun and Creole music, and a major influence on Canray Fontenot and Bois-Sec Ardoin, both of whom played with him when they were young. Bois-Sec's first music lesson was playing triangle behind Amede—the whole time watching his cousin and learning his tunes. "It won't be long before I catch up with you," he once bragged to Amede.

Amede Ardoin was also a close friend of Adam Fontenot, and one of Canray's favorite stories involves a memorable entrance the accordionist made at a local house dance. "Nonc Adam" was playing a dance at his grandfather's house, he recalls, and "when he came back my daddy was playing, and he took his left hand off the accordion, and Amede slapped his in there, then took his right hand, and the tune never stopped! My daddy went in the kitchen, but the people never stopped dancing, they never noticed they had exchanged the accordion. How can that player do something like that?"

There was no such job description as a professional musician in Amede Ardoin's time—except for Amede Ardoin, whose music was favored by both whites and blacks. "He never married, he didn't want to work," says Canray Fontenot. "Amede would put his accordion in that sack and every day Amede would get to the gravel road with his accordion, hitchhike, and he didn't give a damn which direction it was—he'd go somewhere where he could pick up a few nickels."

For a little man, says Fontenot, Amede Ardoin "had a lot of nerve." His ability to compose new songs on the spot is one possible reason for his widespread unpopularity: "Some of them fellas, them and their wife was in a feud or something, and Amede would go sit there and play, and he'd sing about a certain thing the man done to his woman. And whoever it was, they knew what he was thinking about, and they didn't like it. Said he had a bad mouth."

By the end of his life, Amede Ardoin had made enough enemies that he was risking his life whenever he performed. "One time they had a dance hall in Basile," remembers Fontenot, "and what saved him was some white guy who was learning how to play the guitar. Somebody threw a big ol' rock—whoever done it wanted to hurt him bad—and the guitar player put this guitar in front of Amede, and the rock went though the guitar. But you know, he would take chances, and what he done, they kept on hiring him. They went and took some chicken wire and they made a pen there, and they would go get Amede, and they had a bunch of men walking around him, and he would get in the pen there, and he would play anyway."

Along with the music, the tragic story of Amede Ardoin's life has passed into legend, resonating across generations of musicians in Louisiana. It was during a Sunday dance that Ardoin accepted a handkerchief from the white daughter of his boss, Celestin Marcantel. This didn't please at least two onlookers, and the accordionist was severely beaten later that night. According to Fontenot and Ardoin, he never quite recovered from the assault, and he died several years later in a mental institution in Pineville. The story of his life has since served as a cautionary tale told by parents to their children, to explain the pitfalls of picking up an instrument.

He made his living inventing and playing his music. He traveled to New Orleans and New York to record his songs. But he stumbled on the tightrope that Creoles walked between black and white. For young musicians looking for role models, Amede Ardoin was, as Canray Fontenot puts it, "both a good example and a bad example."

Bois-Sec and Canray

Bois-Sec Ardoin and Canray Fontenot began playing together at an early age, performing for house dances, at community dance halls, and even for a local live radio broadcast. In 1948 they formed the Duralde Ramblers, playing the songs of Amede Ardoin and Adam Fontenot, and Canray Fontenot reworked a tune he had heard from Douglas Belair into what would eventually become his signature song, the gracefully desolate "Les barres de la prison."

Heeding Amede Ardoin's mistakes, the musicians paid attention to the social customs that regulated Creole dance halls of the day. "Oh, they had all kinds of crazy rules," remembers Fontenot. "When they had a dance, that was for the young people—the old men, they'd head to the barn and play cards and drink and talk while the young people was dancing." The dance was closely chaperoned by the women of the community, Fontenot recalls, who kept close eye on the dancers to make sure they "left a gap."

There were different rules in each community about jackets and short sleeves, and it was expected that young men would wrap a handkerchief around their hand so they wouldn't soil their partner's dress. But even stricter than the rules governing behavior were those minding the music.

Fontenot and Ardoin knew an older fiddler in the area who insisted on playing the blues, and so was barred from house dances for performing that "saloon music." Blues, it seems, was the quickest way to close that respectable gap between dance partners, and it was not allowed in the house unless the clever musicians could find a way to sneak it in.

"You was out of business if you played blues," says Fontenot. "That's where me and Bois-Sec got the idea of 'Bonsoir Moreau,' it's kind of blues—you could kind of slip on them with something they could waltz—you could blues it or you could waltz it. You could play that all night if you wanted."

When Bois-Sec Ardoin is asked about "Bonsoir Moreau," he leaves his seat for the first time during the interview. "This is what they'd dance to it," he explains, taking three steps across the floor of his son's living room, stomping his foot down and taking three steps back. "That's what you call the baisse-bas," he says.

"Them old people—when they'd get to the third step there, they'd stomp that foot down, man they'd make an echo on that old house floor. It'd rock like that. But they're all gone," adds Morris Ardoin.

The Creole music of the Fontenots and the Ardoins, with its remarkable diversity, was once accompanied by an equally wide plurality of dances like the baisse-bas. One early accordionist, Freeman Fontenot, once recounted for interviewer Marc Savoy in *Cajun Music: A Reflection of a People* the various steps you might see in the first half of this century: "No, there was no zydeco long ago. There were ball and jacks, blues, coudinnes, old baisse-bas, the 'tit Moreau, the number nine, shimmy, two cousins, shoo-fly, the fusielle."

As dance styles outpace even clothing fashion, Ardoin and Fontenot provide one of the only continuous links to this rich past, keeping the pair in great demand today with local and international festivals. In addition, Fontenot has recently been reviving his string band repertoire (he once formed a Bob Wills style outfit called the Basile Boys) and has been performing with the Cajun honkytonkers Filé—he celebrated his birthday in Ireland last year with the band.

Many of Ardoin's and Fontenot's Creole songs have also been retooled as zydeco numbers—most recently, young accordionist Geno Delafose recorded Fontenot's "Tes parents ne veulent plus me voir" ("Your Parents Don't Want to See Me Anymore"). Other tunes have been reworked by such acts as John Delafose and Beausoleil.

These new versions of old songs are reminders to Fontenot and Ardoin that popular music in rural Louisiana continues to change around them. Ardoin recalls a time when one son was showing interest in the Cajun rock 'n' roll styles of singer Belton Richard. "That's the style he wanted to play and I stopped him," says Ardoin. "I said take your time with that. You've been raised with that Creole music. We're not going to change it, we're going to stay there. And we stayed there too."

Ardoin has helped train more children and grandchildren than he cares to count but, he says, he can only listen now as the youngest turn to contemporary zydeco. "All my grand-children play zydeco now, but I can't change them," he says, then he laughs.

"Oh no, I got to let them go."

He lets them go because Creole music, like all music, rises from a particular balance of cultures during a certain period of time, one which can't be repeated in quite the same way. Instead, Creole music today hinges on the ongoing relation-ship between its two great players, Canray Fontenot and Bois-Sec Ardoin, who have the kind of alliance in which information can be exchanged in a glance, and on a dime a waltz can be turned into the blues.

"We can read each other's mind," concludes Bois-Sec Ardoin. "It's not like that with anyone else."

Hidden Nation

The Houmas Speak

BARBARA SILLERY

"*When we went to drink at the white water fountain, or tried to go to the white school, they didn't ask us for proof if we are Indian or not. They just said no, go away, you're Indian. Now when we try to get recognized by the Federal government, they say prove to us that you are Houma, that you are Indian.*"
  —STEVE CHERAMIE, Houma Vice-Chairman

"*I consider myself Houma by belief and spirit rather than the amount or percentage of blood that I have running through my veins. To me that is what is important. It doesn't matter what physical features that I have that look Indian. It's what goes on in here.*"
  —JOE DARDARD, Houma Council of Elders

"*A big part of the reason we lost a lot of our Indian heritage and Indian culture was not that the people were not proud they were Houma, but it was a way of protecting their children and so they didn't pass on the traditions, the heritage, and that sort of thing because they were trying to fit them into a white society so that they would be adopted. They didn't want their children to grow up with the prejudices that they grew up with.*"
  —BRENDA DARDAR PITRE, Houma Council Member

They meet at the Tribal Center in Golden Meadow, Louisiana. Angry adult voices fill the former settlement schoolhouse. The raised single-story white framed cottage stands a few hundred feet from the slow moving waters of Bayou Lafourche, just before it empties into the Gulf of Mexico. The swings in the playground hang limply in the humid air as the glare from the sun bounces harshly off the whitewashed

From *Louisiana Cultural Vistas* (Fall 1994): 46–51. Reprinted by permission of the author.

tombs lying nearby. They gather to fill out forms, trace their lineage and prove their "Indianness" to a government only a fraction as old. The people of the United Houma Nation own neither the building they meet in, nor the sacred burial mounds where their ancestors rest. Despite 300 years of recorded history during the white man's reign, the Houmas have failed in their attempts to gain Federal recognition. Their petition before the Bureau of Indian Affairs remains in limbo.

The Houmas believe they are the first people of the land known today as the State of Louisiana. Their ancestors were the Chakchiuma, a Yazoo River tribe, part of the great Muskogean Nation. As early as 1682 the French explorer René Robert Cavelier, sieur de La Salle, noted the presence of a Houma or "Oumas" village. This first white contact occurred on the east bank of the Mississippi as it curves to meet the Red River. Subsequent Spanish governors of the Louisiana territories had numerous dealings with this powerful, yet peaceful tribal group. Both the French and the Spanish acknowledged the Houma's sovereign domain through the exchanging of gifts and the smoking of the calumet.

On March 20, 1699, Pierre Le Moyne, sieur d' Iberville, reported, "I have visited an Ouma settlement . . . with 350 warriors. I was welcomed by the tribe's chief and witnessed dances and celebrations at the village. We smoked the calumet and received gifts of bread, flour and corn." The French explorer was accompanied by Jesuit priest Fr. Jacques Gravier, who wrote extensively in his journal about the lifestyles of those who lived on the banks of the great river: "The calumet was among the North American Indian the mysterious symbol of honor and sworn faith. Scepters and crowns in their day were never the object of more sincere or more deserved respect. In the memory of man, the faith of the calumet was never violated." This unfortunately did not hold true for long.

In 1800, Spain transferred Louisiana to France, and three years later Napoleon sold the territory to the United States. While under Spanish control, Houma land and rights were protected, and it was assumed tribal rights would continue to be guaranteed by the United States. They were not. Article Six of the Louisiana Purchase of 1803 states, "The United States promises to execute such treaties and articles as may have been agreed upon between Spain and the tribes and nations of Indians, until by mutual consent of the United States and said tribes and nations, other suitable articles shall have been agreed upon." Historically, mutual consent rarely included the voices of Native American people. In this case, the Houmas were no different.

Agents of the newly emerging American government reported to President Thomas Jefferson that the Houma people disappeared into the mists of time; therefore, the United States was free from any entanglements with this nonexistent nation. "There are but a few Houmas living on the east side of the Mississippi river, but they scarcely exist as a nation," reported Louisiana Indian Agent John Sibley, 1806. These reports of the Houma Nation's nonexistence were accepted as gospel well into the 20th century. Houma Tribal Chairman Laura Billiot tells a different story: "When they'd take the census, they'd come and check a place out and then say, okay there's nobody there. They were scared to go back there because they knew they had Indians back there and you can talk to any of the old people and they'll tell you that."

A Peaceful and Unnoticed People

Today the tribal rolls of the United Houma Nation list 17,000 men, women, and children. Where do they come from, these people who do not exist? Perhaps paralleling their creation story and their tribal symbol, the red crawfish, the Houmas dug another tunnel up from the underworld and they then stood up and took their place in the world. Like that of thousands of other native people, the Houma story of survival is not as smoothly woven as that of legend or myth. Houmas never engaged in battle with the successive colonial powers of France, Spain, and England who came to rule their land.

Ironically this desire for peaceful coexistence placed the Houmas in virtual obscurity. Without war, there was no need for a written treaty. Without signed documents, there was no official proof of Houma existence. Without proof, it was easy for others to move in and claim title to Houma lands. Where once self-sufficient Houma ancestral villages dominated the bluff lands in the Feliciana parishes of northern Louisiana, now the State Penitentiary at Angola occupies this natural fortress. Today Houma settlements cling precariously to small strips of land amid the inland marshes and swamps of southernmost Louisiana.

It has been suggested that the Houmas cooperated in their own disappearance. Rather than become embroiled with the warring French, Spanish and British factions, Houmas moved farther and farther south. Disease and the encroachment of white settlers added to their losses. Salvation was sought in isolation. Living in palmetto huts on the fringes of the world—Dulac, Bayou Dularge, Isle a Jean Charles—all outward symbols of their "Indianness" removed, the Houmas became an invisible people. Hidden to the outside world, the tribe escaped the forced march along the infamous "Trail of Tears." Their official non-status was also the instrument of their survival. But the price for that survival has been high; their children and their children's children continue to pay.

Much of Houma culture and tribal ways are lost. The elders speak to one another in French, the language of the bayous; the children speak English. The cadence of their parents maintains a mixture of both. They use Christian first names given to them by the priests and missionaries who came to "bring civilization to the savages." Dardar, Verrett, Billiot, Dion, Courteaux, Parfait: these are some of the more common French surnames adopted by the tribe in the 1700s as the French explorers and fur traders married into Houmas clans. After that initial intermarriage with outsiders, Houmas typically married within the tribe.

Occasionally a door to the past slides open, allowing the smallest wisp of memory to filter in. Four generations live at the home of Mary Verrett on the edge of Bayou Dularge. Over the years the simple wood dwelling has grown haphazardly in scattered directions—a bedroom here, a kitchen there. The furniture has settled into comfortable grooves. There is warmth and laughter and occasional jokes about the last ferocious visitor known simply as "Andrew." But even a hurricane, dumping water and mud halfway up her walls, cannot budge Houma Indian Mary Verrett from the only land she has ever known. Here this tiny matriarchal leader of the Verrett clan continues to care for her family. She weaves stories accompanied by the ceaseless motion of her hands stirring a pot of gumbo or sewing clothes for her Spanish moss dolls. Her memories are freeform, a poetry of the heart: "My old grandmother used to tell me some Indian words. She was 107 when she passed on. My Mama, she could sing and she'd dance the Indian dances. They'd make a big fire . . . and they would sing a song they called 'Ah-dee-oh.' She used to dance with them when she was a little girl. I forgot about that, but sometime it come back to you."

In outward appearance, the Houmas assimilated and adapted so well that reclaiming their heritage is a formidable task, a task so painful, some question its value. Even among immediate family members there is not always accord. Seventy-year-old boatbuilder Lawrence Billiot, his face and hands etched with the proud scars of his craft, would prefer not to stir up old wounds. Denying his Indian heritage, if he must be labeled, he insists he is Mexican. His sister, nationally known Houma artist Marie Dean, has been recognized by the Smithsonian for her artistry in preserving the Houma craft of woven palmetto baskets. They do not discuss their differing views on a common heritage. Convincing the elders that there is nothing more to fear is just one of the tribe's many challenges. Adapting to the twentieth century has not been easy. Many question how the Houmas of today are related to the history and culture of the Houma Nation of 300 years ago. Some even question if the Houmas are Indians at all. They are identified as racially hybrid, not fitting into either the white or black communities.

A weathered, blue-shingled, one room grocery store is the only commercial establishment on Isle a Jean Charles, a thin strip of land rapidly losing ground to the onslaught of erosion wrought by pipeline canals and hurricanes from the Gulf of Mexico. The simple store serves the needs of the island's

Indian inhabitants, who have no way of getting to nearby towns. Owner Gus Dardar recalls the effects of discrimination: "In town, I go to a restaurant. They say, 'I don't want you here.' Go to a barber shop, they say 'We can't cut your hair, you're Indian.' When I was a young kid I was treated worse than a dog on the street because I was an Indian. They used to say, 'Look at that little mixed breed out there, that little sabine.' One day I was working on a tugboat and a man called me 'sabine' and I hit him right there and knock him out cold. When he get up, I asked him, 'You want some more?' he said no. He was a bigger man than me and I knock him out cold. I said, 'Anytime you want to call me sabine, I show you.' I fight more than one time for my Indian blood. I'm not ashamed of it and I thank the good Lord quite a bit if one day the Houmas can be recognized to show what we suffered for."

"Sabine" is the worst racial slur that can be thrown at a Houma. Tribal Council member Brenda Dardar Pitre explains: "I am sure other nationalities have their words and that's the word for the Houmas. The greatest insult you can give is to call us sabines. It means referring to us as anything but an Indian; it means we are supposed to be this lower class of person, this mixed breed." Youth Council leader Kevin Billiot agrees: "A lot of people say, that doesn't go on much. That's not true. Maybe not in a city like New Orleans as much as over here. In New Orleans, there are so many people, so many nationalities. Here in Terrebonne Parish in a small town, the people know you. It still goes on."

A major stumbling block for the Houmas has been their denial of their basic right to an education. The testimony of Houma elders is a cruel litany:

> "We were not allowed to go to school in Golden Meadow. They called us black people, niggers is what they called us."—Ophelia Billiot.
> "I don't have no education. I don't have no education at all. I couldn't go to school. I got 84 years old now. Too late to go."—Frank Naquin.
> "We couldn't go. They didn't want to send us with the white. They didn't want to send us with the colored, so we stayed zero."—Hilda William Naquin.

Joe Dardard, another respected Houma elder, is one of the few who not only made it through high school, but continued on to college. His family left Isle a Jean Charles in lower Terrebonne Parish and moved to Jefferson Parish where Houmas could enter the regular public school system. Joe remembers what it was like on the island: "I think one of the sore points of my youth and the people of my generation and the next generation after, was the fact that Houmas were not allowed in public school in Terrebonne Parish. The only thing I could count on was missionary instructors . . . and of course it was considered unofficial because it was not recognized by the school board. If you tried to transfer to another school for instance, the credits were not any good."

The Civil Rights Act of 1964 forced state and local officials to integrate Houmas into the regular public school system. Integration was slow and painful according to Houma Clyde Dion: "My father was one of them that fought for education for forty Indians in Terrebonne Parish. When I went to school, I was one Indian boy among nine Indian girls to go into an all white school. And that's how we infiltrated Terrebonne Parish."

Now that the public school doors are open to the younger generation, which is more sophisticated in its understanding of its rights, the Houmas have renewed their efforts to reclaim title to their lands. Without the right to live and work in the coastal marshes, they cannot survive. The Houmas dispute oil and gas companies' title to more than 600,000 acres of Louisiana wetlands they obtained in 1921. The courts have upheld the claims of the oil and gas companies. Houmas say this is Native land, theirs since the days of their last great matriarchal leader, Rosalie Courteaux. Joe Billiot feels strongly, as others in the tribe do, that his people were misled. "The problem is that they (the Houmas) didn't speak English to begin with. They could not understand the language. They could not read the paper they were asked to sign, because they were uneducated. They took advantage of them by their ignorance." Houma Joseph Verdin echoes these sentiments: "We're at the end. We can't take no more. Now we are willing to die for our right."

It is an ongoing, frustrating battle, a legal battle few Houmas can afford to wage. As a people, the only tribal property owned by the Houmas is another former settlement schoolhouse in Montegut. Their sacred burial grounds are in the hands of others. There is no Houma reservation, although there are many cities, towns, and areas in Louisiana that owe their origins to the Houmas, including Baton Rouge, the state capital. Prior to the arrival of the Europeans, Baton Rouge was Houma hunting grounds. This area was marked by a red stick, standing some thirty feet high, adorned with the heads of fish and bears. It was during this period, shortly before 1692, that these same Houma hunting grounds were invaded by the Bayougoula Indians. There arose among the Houma a legendary female war chief who led her people to victory over the Bayougoulas. She is also referred to in Father Gravier's journal. This female war chief pledged that the red stick, translated by the French into Baton Rouge, would forever mark Houma territory. Sadly this too became another unfilled prophecy. Louisiana's state capital retains this Houma place name, along with the city of Houma, Houmas Point, Houmas House and other former Houma sites.

In 1972, recognizing the plight of all Louisiana Indians, Governor Edwin Edwards established two agencies to assist Indian communities on the state level, the Office of Indian Affairs and the Intertribal Council. In 1977, the State of Louisiana officially, if belatedly, acknowledged the existence of the Houma people, making them one of nine Louisiana tribes with state recognition and limited rights. Edwards urged the federal government to do the same. Although the Houmas are the largest of these tribes, the federal government has to date recognized only three of these tribes: the Chitimacha, Coushatta (Koasati), and the Tunica-Biloxi. In dispute are several federal criteria such as the continuity of the tribal leadership. The stakes being played for include, on the one hand, the simple question of legitimizing their identity and, on the other hand, also at stake are various federal grants and entitlements reserved for recognized tribes.

In 1979, to meet criteria set forth by the Bureau of Indian Affairs, the tribe incorporated into a legal entity the

United Houma Nation. Rather than chiefs governing individual Houma settlements dispersed throughout the marshland, the Houmas organized themselves into a centralized councilmanic form of government. To meet federal criteria, today they govern themselves through a 14-member elected council, officers and a Tribal Chairman, Laura Billiot. The council represents Houmas residing in the main areas of Terrebonne, Lafourche, Jefferson, St. Mary and St. Bernard parishes as well as those living outside these districts. However, conforming to another society's standards does not guarantee unity. As the Houmas enter their Era of Change, the transition between traditional and modern methods is not always harmonious. Houmas of the twentieth century no longer live in the palmetto huts of their ancestors, nor are all tribal members comfortable with the outward vestiges of Native American ways.

Recent powwows have focused on a blending of both worlds. Grayhawk Perkins, a cultural humanist and Houma Tribal member, organized the first annual Houma Calumet Powwow at the Louisiana Nature and Science Center in 1992 where Houmas celebrated their heritage together with other southeastern tribes. Open to the general public, the Powwow now regularly held in May allows visitors to learn and share Houma culture. March of 1994 witnessed the revival of another traditional Houma Powwow. Last held in 1987 at Grand Bois Park in Bourg, Louisiana, the Calling of the Tribes Pow Wow held special significance for many in attendance. Morning Dove, Mary Verrett Cashmere, was chosen as the Head Lady Dancer. She is the granddaughter of the late medicine man (traiteur) Howard Parfait and medicine woman (traiteuse) Eleven Lucy Parfait. In her hair she wore an eagle feather, perhaps the single greatest honor that can be bestowed on a Native American. During the intertribal dancing on Saturday afternoon, a bald eagle was observed soaring over the dancers, then returning to his nest in a towering cypress tree.

Houmas are hopeful that perhaps this singular honor is symbolic of a more rewarding future for the tribe. For the Houma people, all life is a circle; within the circle of time, the inner core of Houma identity, with or without federal recognition, lives on.

Some Accounts of Witch Riding

Patricia K. Rickels

At the time of the New England witch trials, no charge was more common than that the accused had "ridden people," that is, leaped upon them as they slept and "grievously oppressed them."[1] The word *nightmare*, commonly used today to mean merely a bad dream, is also defined by *The American College Dictionary* as a "monster or evil spirit formerly supposed to oppress persons during sleep." Here the word *formerly* implies that witchriding is extinct in America. The fact that it survives in American Negro folk tradition is recognized by Richard Dorson when he speaks of "the luminous ghosts who alarm colored folk at dusk dark, and the shape shifting witches who straddle them in bed."[2] That it survived among Louisiana Negroes a generation ago is attested by two brief mentions of witch riding in *Gumbo Ya Ya*.[3] The accounts presented here will demonstrate that the belief is still both widespread and deeply entrenched among Negroes in the French-Catholic culture area of southwestern Louisiana.

At the suggestion of Wayland Hand, president of the American Folklore Society, I began in 1958 to collect folklore from my students at the University of Southwestern Louisiana. Such a project is bound to be full of surprises; my first was discovering a student who had been ridden by a witch.

A serious-minded Negro in his mid twenties, a native of Abbeville, a Catholic, he speaks both French and English. His full account is given below, just as he wrote it, because he

From *Louisiana Folklore Miscellany* 1:2 (1961): 1–17. Reprinted by permission of the author.

represents a paradox perhaps not found in America since the seventeenth century. Like Cotton Mather,[4] he is intelligent, literate, sophisticated about most things, but full of a simple faith in the "wonders of the invisible world," wonders which he describes in direct, concrete, and often colloquial language, though employing generally a finished prose style.

Prologue

Few people are willing to admit that superstition has some truth in it. Those who believe in such far fetched ideas are regarded as ignorant. Whether I am called ignorant or not, I do believe to a greater degree than most people. I have good reason to believe in witches, however, as you will discover when you read this story. The story is true, believe it or not, as you may.

The Ride of the Witch

My grandfather was regarded as the best storyteller in our community. Almost every night the boys and girls in our neighborhood would assemble in the parlor of our home to listen to the old man.

One evening, while grandfather was in the midst of about ten small children and getting ready to begin his session of storytelling, I tip-toed into the room inconspicuously, for I did not want to interrupt his guests. In the meantime, he had begun to tell the tale of the witch. He described her as being tall and bony. She had a mouth almost bare of teeth, with the exception of one long tooth in the center of the upper part of her bridge; a long nose with several pimples scattered around and near the tip; long, gray, stringy hair which resembled the threads of a soiled mop; fingernails about an inch long, and a complexion as white as a sheet. She was attired in a dingy black dress and wore a pointed black hat.

Grandfather went on to say that her evil duty, among others, was to sneak into the homes of bad boys and girls and haunt them while they slept. This occurred usually after midnight when she was certain that everyone was asleep.

This is how she went about her task of haunting; first, after entering a home, she would go from room to room in search of a victim to ride, but the only way she could ride the victim was to find him sleeping on his stomach; second, if the conditions were contrary to her expectations, she would then use force to roll the sleeping person over. The moment the witch rolled him over, she would pounce on his back and ride the daylights out of him. This was surely an experience he would never forget.

The only way to get her off your back was to pray, said grandfather. The witch was afraid of prayers. If one had the power to make the sign of the cross or utter a prayer, she would immediately leave the house. The prayers, however, had to be heard by the witch or otherwise they were of no use. She fought with all her might to prevent the mere thought of someone saying a prayer.

After grandfather had finished telling spine-tingling tales, the children were too afraid to go to their homes. It was dark, and they were afraid that the witch would attack them if they dared to venture alone in the night. He told them that if they would run fast and make a lot of noise the witch would not attack them; so finally they decided to leave. You should have seen them run. We could hear their noise blocks away.

I retired to my room and prepared for bed, but after putting out the light, I could imagine that I was seeing all sorts of eerie things around my room. Then I saw something weird coming toward me, crouching and lifting its arms high above its head. It was the witch! She made a wild leap for me, clutching desperately for my head; made a loud screeching noise which sounded like the noise of a bird of prey, preparing to attack its victim. I screamed! I immediately pulled the blankets over my head in a vain attempt to blot out the vision of that horrible creature. But she kept diving in on me, again and again. She tried with all her strength to roll me over, but she could not manage to do it. The bed was wet with the sweat from my body as I lay there helpless and pleading.

Several hours later, when everything had quieted down, the witch led me to believe that she had gone. I was too scared to believe that she had really left the room, and too tired to uncover my head. So, I remained motionless under the blankets until I could find strength to move the tired muscles in my body.

My weariness led me into a deep slumber, and somehow, during a bad dream I happened to roll over on my stomach and she hopped me just as fast as ever. Realizing that in my position I could not defend myself, I resorted to making outcries for help, but no one heard me, because no matter how wide I opened my mouth to yell, no sounds would come out of me. If you could but imagine how horrible a situation such as that could be, you would pray that this would never happen to you.

Two nights of those vicious attacks by the witch and I was almost a nervous wreck. In the meantime, however, I had told my mother about all the things that had happened to me. My mother was despondent and she did not know what to do. I begged for her help, but did not know what possible assistance she could give me, except perhaps, to keep a constant watch over me during the nights that followed.

On the third night the witch jumped me again, but that time I gave her a run for her money. I fought her like a savage with all the strength I could muster, but I could not shake her off of my back. She pinned my arms to my sides and used them as reins to subdue all the fight within me. I made a vain attempt to pray out loud, but that only provoked her to a greater degree of contempt for me. She became more violent than ever, and rode me completely out of my bed onto the floor; then steering me toward the stairs, she proceeded to guide me to the very top. There was an opened window, screenless, just above the landing. Her intention was to ride me completely out of the house through that window. Death loomed over me like a dark cloud, waiting cautiously to engulf me. I did not want to die and I pleaded with her to set me free. But she was determined to take me with her. Her mind was made up and there was nothing I could do or say to change it.

Meanwhile, my mother had pulled a bed check on me. When she could not find me in bed she began a mad search through the house for me. By the time she found me I was almost ready to jump out of the window. Upon seeing this, mother became almost hysterical; screaming at the top of her voice she came running to aid me, and reached me in the nick of time, for a minute more and I would have been a goner.

As I stood there staring blankly into space, Mother held my hands and cried piteously, for the witch had almost cost me my life. Now I am a grown man and I am still plagued by the witch. However, through experiences I have learned to cope with her. That is, I don't sleep on my stomach any more. And if I have occasions to roll over during a bad dream, and she should hop on me, well, the story is different now. I have found the strength to make the sign of the cross and utter a vociferous prayer.

I asked this man why the witch chose him to ride. His answer was, "The only reason I know is that I was sleeping on my stomach." I asked him whether he had ever told the priest about the witch. "No," he replied, "I never thought about mentioning it to my confessor."

This turned out not to be an isolated case. When my American literature class next read Cotton Mather's account of Bridget Bishop, I asked whether the stories of her riding people reminded them of anything they knew. Everyone looked blank except the one Negro in the class—a French major, an ex-seminarian, and an excellent student. He said, "Why, it sounds like *cauchemar.*" He went on to explain that he knew people who believed in a spirit that rode sleeping persons and agreed to make inquiries about it in his home town, St. Martinville, Louisiana. The following is his English version of a story told to him in French by an eighty-six-year-old Negro woman, a native of St. Martinville.

"My husband had been living a bad life. A bad woman called Big Marie had hoodooed him[5] in his coffee. He stopped going to church and would come home after twelve almost every night. I knew that he was coming from Big Marie's house, so I would make him sleep alone in another room. One night I heard him straining and coughing and trying to call for help. I lit the lamp and ran to his room. He was trying to push someone away from him."

"I knew that Cauchemar must have had him. So I turned him on his side. Soon as I turned him on his side, Cauchemar left him. So he tried to show me that Cauchemar was leaving out of the door, but only he could see him, I could not. I told him to say his prayers and go back to sleep, but he was too scared to sleep. He sprinkled holy water all around his bed and spent the whole night with the lamp lit."

"What do you think would have happened if you had not waked your husband?" I asked. "Cauchemar would have choked him to death," she replied. Upon being asked if she knew of anyone whom Cauchemar had choked to death, she said that many people who are thought to have died in their sleep of natural causes were in reality strangled by Cauchemar.

"Do you know of anyone else who was caught by Cauchemar?" I asked. "That used to happen to a lot of people a long time ago," she replied. "But people have screen doors today. And, you see, Cauchemar has to count every little hole in the screen before he can enter the house. If he makes a mistake he has to start all over again. That's why he doesn't bother people any more."

"Did he ever bother you?" I questioned. "Oh, yes," she said. "But as soon as I feel him getting on me from my feet, I just turn on my side and he leaves me alone."

"Why doesn't he bother you on your side?"

"I don't know, but he can only catch you when you are lying on your back. If you are fast enough you can roll on your side before he gets a good grip on you and he will have to go."

"But what does he do? How does it feel when he is at you? Does he touch your whole body?" She paused in amazement at my apparent ignorance.

"Oh, yes, he touches you all over even your head. In whatever position he finds you, he will try to hold you. If he gets a good grip, no matter how hard you try you cannot move. You may try to scream, but no

sound comes out. Sometimes when he would catch my
brother, my brother would strain so much that his neck
would be stiff the next day. That's why it's so good to
have someone sleeping with you, so he can wake
you up."

We might note here in passing that just about everybody
in this family was witchridden at one time or another.

Still another student in another class had something to
report. This one, an eighteen-year-old Catholic Negro girl
from Carencro, Louisiana, says she understands French but
cannot speak it. She wrote the following account in a reme-
dial English course.

One night a friend of mines came to my house to sleep
with me. During the middle of the night it seemed as
though I had awaken and heard a voice through the
window, which was up, asking a question in a soft voice
"Which one it is?" I tried to call my mother but the
words couldn't come out. All I could have done was stay
in one place and tremble. A few minutes after I heard the
voice again asking the same question. After I really woke
up I started thinking that it must have been a *Quesma*[6]
because I was sleeping on my back and when I heard the
voice I couldn't get up or call anybody. That happened
about three summers ago.

My white students do not seem to know this tradition,
though they are ready enough to report their beliefs in other
supernatural phenomena. One Youngsville, Louisiana, girl
does remember her grandfather's speaking of *cauchemar* as "a
spirit that colored people believe in." And among Negroes
around Lafayette, the belief persists everywhere. I asked two
older colored persons and both of them were full of information. The first is a woman of about fifty who has lived
all her life in Breaux Bridge, Louisiana, speaks English and
French with equal ease, and can read and write fairly well.
She works as a servant, her husband as a carpenter's helper,
and between them they maintain a high standard of living,
sending all their children through high school and some on
to college. She is not sure whether *cauchemar* is anything more

than a bad dream but is inclined to believe, because she has had other experiences with the spirit world. For instance, her mother, when she had been dead for twenty-two years, once got into bed with her and her husband. They could not see her but could touch her and hear her voice. "*Cauchemar*," she says, "is the spirit of an unbaptized person that chokes you in the night. It comes to scare Catholics who need to go to Communion. It happens when you are lying on your back." "If it happened to you, would you tell the priest," I asked. "Oh, no," she replied. "Those priests don't like hoodoo! They're always talking against it. They say if you fool with hoodoo, you're fooling with the devil. Just last week the priest said, when he preached the Gospel, 'All you peoples that got a dime in your leg[7]—that's hoodoo!' All the people laughed, because plenty of them got a dime in their leg right then! No, ma'am, I wouldn't tell that priest anything—just go on to Communion." (Notice here the curiously confused theology: a spirit sent, presumably by God, for the edification and reformation of the victim, is at the same time interpreted as a manifestation of voodooism, forbidden by the Church.) I read her the account of one of Bridget Bishop's victims, written down in Salem, in 1693, and she approved it as "Just right." When I told her that some of my students believed an attack by the *cauchemar* did not mean you had done anything wrong, she took this as just one more example of the younger generation's flippancy which will bring about their ruin.

I also discussed *cauchemar* with an "old style" Negro, an elderly woman who lives with her tenant farmer husband in the country, near Milton, Louisiana, has no new-fangled ideas, and has never been to school. She speaks English well but calls herself a Creole. She boasts that she "can't even understand Cajun" but talks "better Creole than Mayor Morrison on T.V." She has had experience with *cauchemar* and knows many others who have also. It is the spirit of an unbaptized person who jumps on Catholics who have been remiss about their prayers. The spirit takes the form of an old gray-haired woman. It is visible only to the victim, whom it attacks when he is in bed but "Cauchemar stops everything." At last one can out wrestle the thing, manage to say a prayer, and hope to avoid further encounters by being faithful in his prayers from then on. I asked her whether a person's leading an immoral life would bring the attack of the spirit. She had never heard of that. I asked if she had ever told the priest about her experience with *cauchemar* and she said, no. I asked whether *cauchemar* was the same as a witch. "Well," she said, rather dubiously, "some peoples calls it a 'wench'." The word was obviously not familiar to her.

Richard Dorson has remarked that some Negro tales of witch riding "strongly echo the Salem witchcraft records of seventeenth-century New England."[8] A number of such resemblances might be cited in the accounts I have collected. The basic similarity is obvious: one of the faithful is attacked in his sleep by a mysterious being who chokes off his breath until repelled by the force of prayer or until a second person takes hold of the victim. And many of the details are strikingly reminiscent of Salem: the appearance as an ugly old woman, the entry through a window, the stopping of the power of speech of the victim, the invisibility of the witch to all but the victim. But the differences from Salem accounts are about as striking. Most important, in New England, the witch was an identifiable person in the community, in league with the powers of evil. From this fact arose the whole quality of the witchcraft cases in Salem. They were matters of public interest, ecclesiastically and legally. There was a criminal to be brought to justice under the edict "Thou shalt not suffer a witch to live." The accounts I have presented clearly show *cauchemar* to be unconnected with persons known to the victim. It may be a good, rebuking spirit or a bad, malicious spirit. But it is a spirit, not a person in league with the devil. Thus there is no legal problem. The experience is a private one, so private that even one's priest is not ordinarily told of it, much less an officer of the law. There are other notable differences from the Salem pattern. The emphasis placed by all my informants on the importance of the position of the sleeper has no parallel that I have been able to discover. And this is the one condition insisted upon in all five accounts. Whatever else brings a witch to ride you, you must be lying in a certain position or the spirit will be unsuccessful. There is no mention of shape-shifting or of animal familiars in any of the accounts. The Catholic sacramentals—the sign of the cross, the holy water—are certainly not echoes of Cotton Mather's Salem. One of the most interesting contrasts between Salem and Southwest Louisiana witches is their color. The witches who plagued white New Englanders were often black. The devil was dark-skinned, and so were those who dealt with him.[9] Conversely, the witch who rides Louisiana Negroes is white. The sociological implications here may be illustrated by the remark of a New Orleans Negro quoted in Gumbo Ya Ya: "I seen plenty of witches, too. Them things ride you at night. . . . I think lots of white peoples is witches. Others is just plain bitches."[10] Finally, we might note the enormous difference in emotional attitude between the witch-ridden of seventeenth-century Massachusetts and twentieth-century Louisiana. Hysteria was the order of the day there and then. Yet only a few persons were bewitched in New England, whereas many in Louisiana seem to be troubled by cauchemar at one time or another. And we cannot quite accept the view expressed by Christina Hole that "today what was once a universal creed has, for most people, sunk to a shamefaced and only half-acknowledged superstition, shorn of its worst terrors, and never again . . . to influence our lives in any serious manner."[11] My informants were not shamefaced, and two of them believe that cauchemar can kill his victim.

Whatever its likenesses to and differences from the classic New England pattern, the witch riding tradition in Louisiana must, like every folk tradition, serve some need in order to survive. Kittredge remarks that all the theology of witchcraft has the same origin: the need to explain bad things that actually happen to people.[12] Cauchemar functions in just this way. It provides an acceptable explanation for otherwise mysterious phenomena: bad dreams, sleepwalking, waking up with a stiff neck, or even death in sleep. Witch riding is adequate as an explanation of all these things. But the motivation of the witch is sketchy in most of these cases. Logically a witch should have a reason for riding a victim. The primary reason in Salem was personal revenge or spite, but the absence here of any attempt to identify the witch with a known person rules out that motive. There was an elaborate mythology connected with witchcraft in Western Europe, and to a lesser degree in England and New England. Both the doctrine of the *incubus* or *succubus* and that of the Witches' Sabbath were apparently related to witch riding. The *incubus*, a male spirit, and the *succubus*, a female spirit, descended on sleeping persons for the purpose of having sexual intercourse with them. There is no direct survival of this belief in local witch riding tales; however, a remnant of the *incubus-succubus* tradition may perhaps be preserved in the insistence on the importance of the position in which the victim lies. Since a man is attacked when lying on his stomach, a woman when lying on her back, this could be a relic of the tradition underlying the etymology of *incubus* (one who lies on) and *succubus* (one who lies under).

A clearer connection may perhaps be made with the Witches' Sabbath. There seems to be a survival in the first account given here of the tradition that witches sometimes use their victims for transportation to the Witches' Sabbath, often, but not always, turning them into horses by means of a magic bridle. The victim recalls: "She pinned my arms to my sides and used them as reins to subdue all the fight within me. . . . She became more violent than ever, and rode me completely out of my bed onto the floor; then steering me toward the stairs, she proceeded to guide me to the very top. . . . Her intention was to ride me completely out of the house through that window." He was afraid for his life, because he assumed he would fall and be killed. Here we have the idea of being ridden like a horse without the logical accompanying idea of a destination which the witch needs a mount to reach. Negro witch-riding stories from other parts of the South often have this element more clearly defined, even when the Witches' Sabbath is not the specific destination. Mark Twain has Jim in *Huckleberry Finn* tell how "the witches bewitched him and put him in a trance, and rode him all over the State, and then set him under the trees again, and hung his hat on a limb to show who done it. And next time Jim told it he said they rode him down to New Orleans; and, after that, every time he told it he spread it more and more, till by and by he said they rode him all over the world, and tired him most to death, and his back was all over saddle-boils. Jim was monstrous proud about it, and he got so he wouldn't hardly notice the other niggers."[13] There is a Virginia Negro ballad about a victim being ridden by witches to a fox hunt.[14] My informant has apparently kept the terminology of mount and rider but not the idea of purpose in the ride beyond mere malice on the witch's part. He has never heard of the Witches' Sabbath as such.

The source of our local witch riding tradition is a complex problem. Dorson insists on a European rather than an African origin on the basis of Christian elements. If we accept this premise, it is still difficult to fix a European source.[15] Spain, England, and France all brought witchcraft with them to the New World. That the belief lingered long in Spanish America is shown by the burning of two witches in Mexico as late as 1874.[16] The Catholicism of southwestern Louisiana seems to argue against penetration of the New England Puritan witchcraft beliefs. It seems most likely that the French brought witch riding to Louisiana as they did that other, and perhaps related, survival from the middle ages, the *loupgarous*, the werewolf of the bayous. And African origin of some aspects of the local tradition cannot be entirely dismissed. The Negroes concerned clearly connect *cauchemar* with voodoo, and their instinct in this may not be altogether wrong, for the African tradition of the *loa* has much in common with *cauchemar*. The *loa* is a spirit which possesses a human being, though usually with his consent and when he is awake. The similar use of equestrian images to express the relation between possessed and spirit is especially striking. The *loa* is said to take a person as a "mount" and to "ride" him.[17] Puckett, in his *Folk Beliefs of the Southern Negro*, notes that "the beliefs relating to burial, ghosts, and witches show certain broad similarities both in Europe and Africa."[18] He believes that Afro-American beliefs result from contact between these two cultures.

The reason why Negroes and not whites preserve the belief may be simple cultural lag, perhaps reinforced by voodooism. Puckett found in his investigation that southern Negroes were "in part, at least, custodians of former beliefs of the whites."[19] Especially among illiterate Negroes in rural areas he discovered many fragments of earlier European thought. The witch-riding tradition, though still a very lively one in our Negro-French-Catholic cultural community, is losing its moral force. The older generation believes *cauchemar* has a real significance: to punish or warn against wrongdoing. The younger generation believes the experience is just something that happens without any real reason or meaning. Probably the next step will be for witches to stop riding altogether.

Notes

1. *Narratives of the Witchcraft Cases, 1648–1706*, ed. George Lincoln Burr (New York: Charles Scribner's Sons, 1914), pp. 225–27 and *passim*.
2. Richard Dorson, *American Folklore* (Chicago: University of Chicago Press, 1959), p. 185.
3. Lyle Saxon and others, *Gumbo Ya Ya* (Boston: Houghton Mifflin Company, 1945), pp. 258, 545.
4. New England Puritan clergyman and author, 1663–1728.
5. Brought bad luck on him by magic means, in this instance by adding a potion to his coffee.
6. Witch.
7. A hole is punched in a dime and it is tied around the leg to ward off illness.
8. p. 185.
9. *Narratives of the Witchcraft Cases*, pp. 261, 298, 312, 326, 344, 355, etc.
10. p. 298.
11. Christina Hole, *Witchcraft in England* (New York: Charles Scribner's Sons, 1947), p. 19.
12. George Lyman Kittredge, *Witchcraft in Old and New England* (New York: Russell & Russell, 1956), pp. 4–6.
13. Chapter 2.
14. R. Meikleham, "A Negro Ballad." *Journal of American Folklore*, VI (1893): 300.
15. p. 185.
16. Henry Charles Lea, *Materials Toward a History of Witchcraft*, ed. Arthur C. Howland (New York: T. Yoseloff, 1939), III, p. 1528.

17. Alfred Metraux, *Voodoo in Haiti*, trans. Hugo Charteris (New York: Oxford University Press, 1959), pp. 120–22. Also, in this connection Newbell Niles Puckett notes that in New Orleans and parts of Mississippi a "voodoo doctor" is sometimes spoken of as a "horse." *Folk Beliefs of the Southern Negro* (Chapel Hill: University of North Carolina Press, 1926), p. 159.
18. p. 165.
19. p. 2.

10

Charlene Richard

Folk Veneration among the Cajuns

MARCIA GAUDET

Charlene Richard, a young Cajun girl who died of leukemia in 1959, is regarded by many in south Louisiana as a saint. Thousands have made pilgrimages to her grave in Richard, Louisiana (a small farming community 35 miles northwest of Lafayette), though there has been no official recognition or investigation by the Catholic church. Because of the beliefs associated with Charlene and what appear to be the beginnings of legend formation, Charlene Richard has become what might be called an indigenous, regional, popular, non-canonized, folk, or local saint.

Though I had grown up in a Catholic family in Louisiana and my sons attended Catholic schools in Lafayette, where we had lived for eighteen years, I was not aware of the devotion to Charlene until June of 1989. At that time, one of my nieces, who also lives in Lafayette, was diagnosed with a potentially life threatening illness. Within a short time, several people had contacted her parents and grandparents (who live near New Orleans) to tell them about Charlene or to send them her prayer card, and even Xeroxed copies of the card. At that time, Charlene was apparently well-known in devout religious circles in Louisiana, but media attention had been primarily through the Catholic press, not the secular media. Shortly before the thirtieth anniversary of Charlene's death, 11 August 1989, there began a remarkable media focus on this local saint, projecting her story far beyond the local area. During that summer, I started collecting information about

From *Southern Folklore* 51:2 (1994): 153–66. Reprinted by permission of University Press of Kentucky.

the devotion to Charlene and interviewed her mother as well as other family members and friends.

In the past, especially before mid-twentieth century, a saint's cult (i.e., a large following of people who share a devotion to a person believed to have special powers of intercession) often formed slowly, spreading from person to person by word of mouth for more than a century. In the case of Charlene, not only has the cult formed quickly, but many people who knew Charlene as an ordinary child are still living. Of importance in considering this contemporary phenomenon are the effects of technology and the media, particularly the secular media, on the formation, expansion, and expression of cult devotion, the role of the clergy in the devotion to Charlene, and the effects of this cult devotion on the Richard family.

The Catholic Encyclopedia defines *saint* as "a title properly given to those human members of Christ recognized by the Church, either traditionally or by formal canonization, as being in heaven and thus worthy of honor" (1967, 12: 852). More simply, sainthood is the state in which an individual, after death, is understood to be in the direct presence of God. Thus, as Stephen Wilson notes in *Saints and Their Cults*, saints are beings whose special virtues and circumstances have made them suitable and powerful mediators between . . . the everyday human world and the distant rulers of the cosmos (Wilson 1983: 2). Wilson also points out that in the early church, all of the faithful were called "saints." During the early persecution of the Christians, the term came to be used only for martyrs. Later, belief in saints as sanctified intercessors and procurers of miracles led to cults of veneration.

While local devotion to many folk saints began during their lifetimes because of religious work or healing (see, for example, Fish 1984; Low 1988; Macklin 1988; Margolies 1988; Slater 1986; and Slater 1990), this was not the case with Charlene. Unlike many other folk saints, Charlene had not been the object of devotion or a folk heroine during her lifetime. However, local cults based on very young individuals who die prematurely are not really unusual. James Griffith's work on the Alta Pimería region includes interesting studies of young victim-intercessors believed locally to behave like saints in granting petitions, and other contemporary unofficial devotional cults (Griffith 1987; 1992).

The stories, veneration, and cult formation regarding Charlene seem to have originated with personal narratives about Charlene told mainly by the nun and priest who attended her at Our Lady of Lourdes hospital in Lafayette, Louisiana, during the days before her death. Stories of her bravery in the face of certain death and her "offering up" of her suffering for others soon spread, with tales of miraculous intercession for both healing and temporal favors.

Charlene Richard was the second of ten children in her family. Within the Cajun community, there was nothing unusual about the little girl or her family. They were hardworking people strongly devoted to their Catholic faith in a culture where unquestioning acceptance in matters of religion was the norm for children, if not for most adults. When Charlene was diagnosed with acute lymphatic leukemia in August 1959, the family turned to the parish priest and the hospital chaplain to tell Charlene about her illness and the prognosis. Though she died two weeks after the diagnosis, her simple acceptance of her fate as God's will and her willingness to pray and "offer up" her suffering for others made a lasting impression on those who were with her during this short time. One priest in particular, Father Joseph Brennan, was impressed with Charlene's faith. A newly ordained priest from Philadelphia, he was the chaplain of Our Lady of Lourdes Hospital, and he visited Charlene daily. When he arrived, Charlene would ask him for whom they were to pray that day. Shortly before her death, Father Brennan told her that a beautiful lady would soon come to take her away to heaven. She replied, "Oh, you mean the Blessed Mother. When she comes, I'll tell her Father Brennan says hello" (Brown 1989: 3) or "When she does, I'll say, 'Blessed Mother, Father Brennan was asking for you'" (Gutierrez 1988: 29).

Another person who was greatly impressed with Charlene's influence is Father Floyd Calais of Lafayette. Though he never met Charlene, he was a close friend of Father Brennan, who told him the stories about her.

According to Father Brennan, the people for whom Charlene prayed while she was dying were either cured or converted to Catholicism before their deaths (Gutierrez 1988: 44). Father Brennan and Father Calais, as well as Sister Theresita Crowley, director of Pediatrics at Lourdes Hospital, told others about this child's acceptance of death and the effect of her prayers. Local people began to pray to her for special favors, and she seemed to help them. Many described having "a feeling of closeness" to her and believed that she had interceded for them. Sister Theresita said, "I can't forget her. I feel her presence. I feel her smile" (Gutierrez 1988: 26). She also said that she prayed to Charlene daily. Other people prayed to Charlene for medical cures, help with marital problems, help with finding jobs, and good weather to save the crops.

The cult of devotion to Charlene formed quickly. According to Mrs. Mary Alice Richard, Charlene's mother, the family first learned of the belief in Charlene's "specialness" in the hospital before she died. While there is no indication of any mass media coverage at that time, certainly the telephone facilitated the local spread of this belief from one community to another, in the same way that it enables the quick spread of rumor and gossip. A funeral prayer card with a picture of Charlene and a prayer for her soul was distributed after her death, a common Catholic practice as a memorial to the deceased. Sometime during the late 1960s or early 1970s, cards with her photograph were published that reflected the belief that Charlene had special powers of intercession. These cards include an intercessory prayer to Charlene and a prayer for her beatification. A series of articles about Charlene published in 1975 in the Lafayette diocesan newspaper, *The Morning Star*, greatly expanded the devotion to Charlene. The articles from *The Morning Star* were collected and published as a booklet in 1979, with the title "Charlene, A Saint from Southwest Louisiana?" This booklet was later updated and expanded to include testimony from over twenty people who believe they have been helped by Charlene's intercession (Gutierrez 1988).

The effect of print and media on saints' legends and cult formation in the modern world has been noted by Lydia Fish

Photograph and prayer card on the tomb of Charlene Richard, 1989. Photo by Marcia Gaudet.

(1984: 31). This effect has become even more extensive today because of the widespread availability of printing services, xerographic copying, and fax machines, in addition to "instant" coverage by satellite telecommunication and Cable Network News. The stories about Charlene's serenity during suffering and her special help to those who seek her intercession spread throughout south Louisiana and beyond. By August 1989, the thirtieth anniversary of Charlene's death, thousands were visiting her grave every year, some individually, others in organized tours. Over five hundred thousand prayer cards with a "Prayer to Charlene Richard" and a "Prayer for Beatification" have been distributed. In August 1989, shortly before the anniversary mass, a feature article in the Sunday Magazine of the *Baton Rouge Morning Advocate* said:

> Many people say she helps them with problems in their lives, even though she's been dead for 30 years. They pray to the little Cajun girl for help with failing marriages, cures for illnesses and acceptance of whatever life throws their way. And they say she comes through for them.
> One couple, kneeling beneath a black umbrella protection against the sun, spent a quiet half-hour with Charlene Marie Richard on a recent summer morning.

They knelt in the green grass beside her marble tomb,
and their lips moved silently to her.

After Lucy Courville rose, she bent and traced her
index finger around the outline of the picture of
Charlene's face, which is mounted on the tomb.
(Brown 1989: 3)

It is significant that in Charlene's case, the stories started not
with the folk, but with the Catholic "establishment." Typically,
church officials tend to discourage a local saint's cult. For
example, Candace Slater's study of stories about a noncanon-
ized saint in Brazil shows much conflict between the people
of Juazeiro and the Catholic hierarchy. Padre Cicero was
"defrocked" before his death in 1934 because of alleged claims
to a miraculous transformation of the host, and official church
policy toward Padre Cicero's cult is still cool (Slater 1986).
Though there is no official recognition or investigation by the
Catholic church, the clergy and religious of Lafayette diocese
have been central to the devotion to Charlene beginning with
the priest and nun who knew her. Soon, however, there was
unofficial recognition and devotion from high-ranking diocesan personnel. For example, Gerard Frey, Bishop of Lafayette
at the time the articles were published in The Morning Star, wrote
in the foreword to the booklet about Charlene: "Those whose
quest for sanctity leads them through a life of difficulty and
pain may find strong identification with the life and death of
Charlene Richard. From a simple lifestyle in rural southwest
Louisiana, Charlene has to this day provided a meaningful
example for many of the faithful who learned of her following
her death in 1959" (Gutierrez 1988: 17).

The thirtieth-anniversary mass commemorating Charlene's
death was celebrated on the grounds of St. Edwards Church in
Richard. Attendance was estimated at four thousand, and the
event was covered by television stations from throughout
Louisiana, as well as CNN. Prominent clergy, including Father
Brennan and Father Calais, were co-celebrants with Harry
Flynn, the Bishop of Lafayette. Bishop Flynn said during the
mass: "A little girl walked among us. She taught us how to
accept disappointment and suffering."

Father Brennan's homily was similar: "We are here tonight to learn what made a little girl from this community thirty years ago die well. We learn tonight a lesson in acceptance. Perhaps we can learn tonight how to handle our own suffering."

Newspapers throughout Louisiana reported on the event. The *Lafayette Advertiser* said the week before: "Richard—They call her the little Cajun 'Saint' although she has not been canonized by the Catholic Church and as yet there has been no official investigation begun on her behalf. But for hundreds, even thousands of faithful who have learned the story of Charlene Marie Richard, the lack of official sanction by the church is just a minor concern" (1989: 5).

Following the mass, the *Baton Rouge Morning Advocate* reported with a front page headline: "Thousands Attend Mass for Charlene." The article went on to say: "With teary eyes and trembling hands they placed flowers on Charlene Richard's grave, some asking for miracles, others expressing thanks to the girl many people think should become a saint" (1989: 1). The article was accompanied by a color photo of a woman in a wheelchair leaning over to touch Charlene's grave. Stephen Wilson notes that cults often center on saints' remains and that visiting and touching the tomb of a person believed to be a saint is a paraliturgical/unorthodox practice associated with cults (Wilson 1983: 11–14). Such stories, illustrated with color photographs, have obvious emotional appeal and can now reach a much wider and much more distant audience.

Since then, there have been feature articles on Charlene in many newspapers in Louisiana and surrounding states, including a front-page story in the *Dallas Times Herald*, as well as a nine-page article in the American Airlines' inflight magazine, *American Way*, in 1991. It is remarkable and somewhat ironic that the journalistic media should give such wide coverage to what was a very local devotion, particularly effective because the child was identified with the area. Though this is not limited to the case of Charlene, the media have the potential of swiftly making a local saint known worldwide. In Charlene's case, this attention started with the Catholic media, but by 1989, the role of the secular media, including

Charlene Richard's grave marker, Richard, 1989. Photo by
Marcia Gaudet.

national television networks such as CNN, became extremely
important. This media attention not only reinforced local
devotion, but made this "local" saint accessible worldwide.
For example, there is reportedly interest in Charlene in the
former Yugoslavia, and there are plans to translate and print
her prayer cards in Croatian. This is possibly also reinforced
by the large number of people from Louisiana who have
made pilgrimages to Medjugorje to visit the site of the
alleged apparitions of the Blessed Virgin Mary. The "interna-
tionalization" of local phenomena by the secular media inadvertently promotes belief and cult formation and potentially
undermines the role of the official Church.

Wilson also points out that saints' cults were traditionally
thought of as belonging to the people, not the clergy (Wilson
1983: 39–40). Devotion to Charlene apparently did not begin
with the folk. It began outside her own immediate community and seemed to be strongly supported by local clergy.
Maurice Schexnayder was Bishop of Lafayette at the time
Charlene died. He had been chaplain at the Catholic Center
at Louisiana State University in Baton Rouge and is perhaps
best known outside of Louisiana as the priest who converted
the poet Robert Lowell and others at LSU to Catholicism.

Charlene Richard's grave, with rosaries left on the statue of the Blessed Virgin Mary. 2001. Photo by Marcia Gaudet.

Bishop Schexnayder is said to have visited Charlene's grave many times. Father Stanley Begnaud, pastor at St. Edward's Church in Richard from 1968 to 1975, said: "I remember we were sitting at the table. . . . During the course of the conversation Bishop Schexnayder said, 'You Italians [a reference to Msgr. Benedict and Fathers Capra and Gremaldi] have your saint in Maria Goretti, but we [a reference to the people of the Lafayette diocese] have our saint in Charlene Richard'" (Gutierrez 1988: 59). Sister Theresita Crowley suggests the role of clergy in comparing Charlene to St. Thérèse of Lisieux, saying, "I think perhaps Charlene is a lot like the Little Flower—in that many priests openly express their belief in her sainthood" (Gutierrez 1988:24).

Both Maria Goretti (1890–1902) and Thérèse of Lisieux (1873–1897), also known as the Little Flower of Jesus, are examples of Roman Catholic girl-saints whose cults formed quickly. They were young women who lived devout lives and died prematurely. Both were canonized in an unusually short time. Maria Goretti was murdered while defending her chastity. The brutality of the crime, her willingness to offer up her sufferings, and the cures and conversions (particularly that of her attacker) attributed to her intercession led to her canonization in 1950, which was attended by her mother as well as her murderer. Thérèse of Lisieux became a Carmelite nun at the age of fifteen and died a painful death from a tubercular condition after offering up her suffering. Her humility and her simplicity in living, explained in her writings as her "little way" of achieving sanctity, led to her canonization in 1925, only twenty-eight years after her death.

Thérèse of Lisieux, the Little Flower, was certainly a model for Charlene as a young girl saint. In Cajun and Creole areas of Louisiana, as in other Francophone regions in North America, devotion to the Little Flower is well established. Many Catholic churches in the area have statues or paintings of her near the altar. In May 1959, Charlene read a "picture story" book about St. Thérèse, the Little Flower. According to her grandmother, Mary Matte, after reading the book Charlene said she wanted to be like St. Thérèse. She asked if she, too, could become a saint, saying, "If I pray like St. Theresa, will it happen?" (Gutierrez 1988: 38).

As the devotional cult formed, Charlene's "merits" or claims to sainthood were sometimes questioned by those who knew her or her family members personally. Some who knew her were quoted as saying, "I knew Charlene, and there was nothing special about her." Over the years, this resulted in conflict in the local community and even ridicule for the Richard family. When they suffered a series of tragedies and misfortunes, some people in the community interpreted the meaning of these events negatively. For example, in 1977 Charlene's brother Gene (who was also her godchild) was killed in an automobile accident. Mrs. Richard thought at the time that she was being punished. She remembers thinking, "My God, what did I do to deserve this?" (1989). Mrs. Richard said that her children at times resented the attention, particularly when they were teenagers. Earline Richard Hollier, one of Charlene's sisters, remembers feeling that they could never live up to what people expected of them (1989).

Mrs. Richard expressed the family's pain and conflict regarding their situation in 1986:

> It has been hard, all these years. I felt angry a lot of times because she's my daughter and they're not leaving us alone. Why can't they just leave us alone? But then I talked to a priest and he said, "She was your daughter while she was on earth, it's true. But now she is in heaven, and she's not just your daughter anymore. Now she belongs to everyone." So now I feel better about it. (Gutierrez 1988: 77)

When a cult of devotion forms for a local or folk saint who has lived a long life, the parents or siblings of the alleged saint would probably not be directly affected by the cult. For example, Slater's study of a nonconsecrated saint from Granada (Hermanico Leopoldo, 1864–1956) shows very different dynamics. Though he died only a few years before Charlene, he had lived a long life as a Capuchin priest and the stories of miracles (and his ability to levitate) were known and told before his death. In addition, since he lived to be ninety-two years old, by the time of his death, none of his immediate family were likely to be living—certainly not his parents (Slater 1990). This is often not the case with very young saints since their families are often alive and even involved in the formation of the cult. The older sisters of Thérèse of Lisieux, particularly Celine Martin (in religion, Sister Genevieve), were active and influential in promoting her cause. This has not been the case with the Richard family, whose role is somewhat ambivalent. Because media coverage often includes information about Charlene's family, many visitors to Charlene's grave also go to visit her mother who lives a few miles away. She has been interviewed many times by reporters, and she has had tour buses drive up to her door. Mrs. Richard feels she has to talk to them. She said, "I always felt I had to talk about her. I couldn't leave her behind. The same thing with my son who got killed." Charlene's brother Dean expresses the caution the family feels they must show to outsiders. He says, "I believe she's in heaven. But whether she was especially chosen by God, I believe it in my heart, but to say I definitely think it's so would open us to ridicule" (M.A. Richard 1989; D. Richard 1989).

Although there was some opposition in the local area to the devotion to Charlene (one person was quoted as saying, "She ain't no saint"), there are many local people who believe she is special. Katie Hensgens, former housekeeper for Father Joe Lafleur, who was pastor of St. Lawrence Church in Mowata (a small community near Richard), said she heard stories "as soon as they started." Father Brennan, she says, promoted the devotion. Ms. Hensgens keeps the prayer card with a picture of Charlene in her wallet, and she reads the prayer to Charlene daily. She believes Charlene is a saint, and like many people, she thinks she will be the first from the Cajun area to be canonized. As an example of Charlene's intercession, Ms. Hensgens said that in 1990, a widow went to Charlene's grave and kneeling before the grave, she began praying to find someone to marry. Still kneeling, she met the man kneeling next to her. They talked for a while and then went into the church to pray. He telephoned her soon after, and a few months later, they were married (Hensgens 1990).

Mrs. Delia Link of Richard is the mother of Lucille Link, who was one of Charlene's closest childhood friends. Mrs. Link also knew Charlene as a student in her catechism class in Richard. She said that she is often asked, "Did you see sainthood?" Her answer is, "No, I didn't. She was just a little girl with my little girl." Mrs. Link has one of Charlene's prayer cards on her bookcase. Looking at the card, she said, "I never dreamed when they were growing up . . ." Mrs. Link related the following story about Charlene's death: "A few days before she died, she called my daughter and said, 'Come and see me.' I'll always remember her this way. She had a pretty little pair of red pajamas. . . . A few days later, she died." According to Mrs. Link, Mrs. Richard later gave her a piece of Charlene's red pajamas as a relic. One Sunday she saw a woman whose young son was very ill crying in church. She had come there to pray. Mrs. Link had the relic from Charlene in her purse and gave it to the mother, who then seemed greatly comforted.

Mrs. Link relates that Charlene sometimes spent the night with her daughter, and she did not seem in any way different. She said, "She had a lot of faith, but she was raised with that background. And she was very smart." Mrs. Link also related how the nuns taught students to "offer it up" when they were sick or suffering or when they were faced with sacrifice or disappointment. They were taught unquestioning faith and acceptance. Mrs. Link does not remember when she first heard that there was something special about Charlene, but she remembers when Father Floyd Calais came to Richard as pastor a few years later. She said, "He was the one who pushed this, I think. He never knew her—came here after she had died." When asked about the reaction in the community, she replied: "They felt as I do. They knew her as a little girl. Of course, I ask her to pray with me, as a lot of people do. As somebody said, if God wants her to be a saint, it will happen." She also stressed that most people in the area do not reject the idea that Charlene is a saint and that local people do visit her grave. For example, she said, a local carpenter prayed to Charlene when his wife was committed to a mental hospital. His wife recovered, and he has great confidence that Charlene helped through her intercession.

Mrs. Link said, "I can't say that I know of any miracles, but people will grab on to anything. People come by the bus loads, from New Orleans and Houston. The media picked it up." Regarding canonization, she says: "Maybe it will happen, but not in our lifetime. I'm sure she's a saint. That's what the church teaches. But canonization—that's something else" (Link 1990).

While early saints could be canonized by local churches and bishops, since A.D. 1234 canonization to sainthood is a power reserved for the Pope. Pierre Delooz, in his study of sainthood, has said, "Sainthood depends on a community's recollections of a dead person's past existence" (Delooz 1983: 194). Value judgments and recollections of the past are presented in narratives about the person's life. Pressure for canonization is expressed through official channels when there is strong enough belief to create a public cult. Delooz also discusses the special criteria for sanctity: writings, heroic virtue, martyrdom, or miracles (Delooz 1983: 202). In Charlene's case canonization will depend on authenticated miracles and on the strength of her devotional cult to pursue documentation. In the Catholic church's two-stage process, beatification and then canonization, two authenticated miracles are required for each stage (*The New Catholic Encyclopedia* 1967, 12: 82–83).

One of the widely known stories about Charlene's intercession, and the case many believe to be a miracle, involves a young child from Morgan City, Louisiana, named Nicole. Though Nicole's physicians have said that the remission of her cancer (neuroblastoma) was a medical cure that required no miracle, her story is often related as an example of Charlene's intercession. According to Nicole's grandmother, the child repeatedly asked for Charlene, though no one had mentioned the name to her. When she showed the prayer card to Nicole, the child allegedly identified the photo as "Charlene." Nicole participated in the 1991 anniversary mass for Charlene, during the Offertory portion of the mass, by carrying the basket containing the written petitions to Charlene up to the altar. In addition, there is a belief that patients who were treated in Room 411 of Our Lady of Lourdes Hospital, the room where Charlene died, always recovered from their illnesses.

Many of the marks of the early cults to the saints remain today and are apparent in the devotion to Charlene. Among them is the belief in the special powers of the saint's remains or objects with which the saint had some contact. Relics from a saint, pilgrimages to the saint's tomb, and images of the saint are often part of the practice of veneration. David Hufford has noted the emphasis in Roman Catholicism on healing and on the meaning of suffering and death, still vigorous today (1985: 194–95). He says, "The traditions of healing among Roman Catholics today are as vigorous as they are ancient . . ." (207). He notes that temporal favors, as well as spiritual favors, are also sought from saints and alleged saints. Petitions to Charlene seldom have to do with spiritual matters or the saving of one's soul. Rather, they deal with health and healing and with practical matters, such as finding jobs, finding mates, and passing exams. Wilson also notes the importance of images of the saints in cults (1983: 15). In the case of Charlene, prayer cards with her picture have been widely circulated at least since 1972 (with the notation, "For Private Devotion only"). Xerographic copies of the prayer cards are often sent to others in need of special help. It is certainly true that south Louisiana is very much given to visible expressions of religion—votive candles, processions, pilgrimages to Medjugorje, St. Joseph's Day altars, yard grottoes, published notices in newspapers of thanksgiving for a favor granted, and so on. The use of votive offerings (*ex voto*) such as flowers, plants, objects, engraved plaques, handwritten notes, pictures, and lighted candles is especially important in devotion to Charlene. Wilson refers to *ex voto* as "authentic popular expression" (1983: 234). In her study of Italian *ex voto*, Elisabetta Galanti says that "the religious custom of offering an object to a divinity 'ex voto suscepto' and putting it in the place dedicated to that divinity has pre-Christian origins" (1988: 79). According to Galanti:

> Votive offerings, or *ex voto*, are not subject to any
> precise ecclesiastical disposition; they are the voluntary
> expressions—private or public, individual or collective—
> of a debt of gratitude to a divinity, either in pursuance
> of a vow for a prayer answered or as a Thanksgiving for
> an unexpected divine intervention. They may take the
> form of an object or an action such as a procession or a
> pilgrimage or the offer may make a gift of himself and
> devote his life to God. (Galanti 1988: 78)[1]

All of these dimensions of *ex voto* are evident in devotion to Charlene as expressions of gratitude or as symbols of special requests. Votive candles are still very popular in rural areas of south Louisiana, and there are votive candles inside the church in Richard. Many people go into the church after visiting the grave to light a votive candle to Charlene. Most *ex voto* offerings, however, are centered upon Charlene's tomb, and the Richard family must again negotiate between their private sensibilities and the public devotion to Charlene. For example, notes and messages have been left on Charlene's tomb for many years, usually weighted down with stones or other objects. The parish now has a padlocked box near the tomb for "Petitions to Charlene." These notes and letters have been collected by the parish priest and brought in boxes to Charlene's mother. Any money left in the petition box is given to the church. Mrs. Richard says that she has many boxes of letters and notes left for Charlene. She does not read them, but she does not feel she can dispose of them either. Engraved metal plaques have also been attached to the tomb without the permission of the family. These also are removed after a time and kept. The family agreed, however, to have the parish build a concrete slab around the tomb to accommodate wheelchairs. Charlene's grave is actually what appears to be a "half tomb," built over her grave. Most of the graves in the cemetery in Richard follow this modified version of burial in above ground tombs, traditional in most of French Catholic Louisiana. Cemeteries in the prairie Cajun region tend to have in-ground burial, with a tomb only a few feet high built over the grave. (The word tomb [in French, la tombe] is commonly used in preference to the term grave.)

Much is traditional in the cult devotion to Charlene, but there are also components that seem to be interesting variations of the route to sainthood, along with new dimensions provided by contemporary technology. It is interesting and somewhat unusual that the local Catholic clergy not only supported the devotion to Charlene, but also seem to have led it. There was also some conflict within the community regarding Charlene, though this was often aimed at the clergy or others, not Charlene. After all, she was only a twelve-year-old child when she died, and she had never claimed any special powers in her lifetime. In addition, there are the effects on her family of the large devotional following thirty-five years after her death. Perhaps most significant is the profound impact of technology and telecommunication on devotion to a "local" saint. Not only are cults formed so quickly that they can have a profound impact on the family and friends of the saint, but the very nature of the hierarchy of steps to recognized sainthood is affected. Folk or local saints have been given private (i.e. not in the church) veneration by local communities, often with no official steps taken toward candidacy for beatification. Those beatified, called "Blessed," are entitled to public veneration locally. Saints are canonized by the Pope and are entitled to universal veneration in the Church. The rapid communication of the contemporary world seems to negate the significance of the "official" requirements of the Church because it is fairly easy to become known far beyond the local community. For example, Charlene has had visitors and letters from places such as Africa and Australia, though she is not yet officially a candidate for beatification. Furthermore, the question of private or public veneration seems moot when the veneration has the support and participation of the diocesan hierarchy and when this veneration is televised on a national news network.

The rapid growth of the devotional cult to Charlene may also reflect the widespread phenomena of belief in angels as celestial messengers in modern life. The need for intermediaries between Heaven and Earth and the "rediscovery" of a higher power is both a popular and scholarly topic (Berger 1970). Charlene can be the equivalent of a personalized angel for the Cajun culture. The fact that she died as a child is important. Her innocence is appealing, particularly at a time when Catholicism in south Louisiana has been recently rocked to its foundations by lawsuits in the 1980s against the Catholic church concerning pedophilic priests. Ironically, such priests were often "hidden" away in rural church parishes. (No such charge, however, has ever been brought against the priests who served in Richard.) The painful need of the Catholic Church in Louisiana to present a more acceptable image is helped by its association with a child saint untouched and untainted by scandal. The devotion to Charlene may reflect a need to return to Catholicism as a central force in the Cajun culture, in spite of widespread anticlericalism and conflict. Jason Berry says in his study of priests and the Cajun culture: ". . . cut off by geography and language from the urban Creole aristocracy, the Cajuns were an insular people, bonded to a code of absolute values: land, faith, and family" (Berry 1992: 6).

These "absolute values" as well as the beliefs, stories, and local conflict about Charlene reflect a basic worldview of the culture of the Cajuns in south Louisiana. Though people disagree on the role of the clergy and on whether Charlene is really a saint with special powers, in times of need they are quite willing to pray to her—just in case she is a saint. This combination of both conflict and acceptance is typical of the practical attitude of the Cajuns about life in general. In addition, there is the definite feeling among the believers that since Charlene is from their own culture, she is approachable and understands their needs.

At this time, Charlene has not yet been beatified—the first step toward canonization, though there are several recorded stories of alleged miracles. Whether she is ever canonized or not, it is likely that the devotion to her will continue in south Louisiana and beyond.

Notes

I presented an earlier, shorter version of this paper at the American Folklore Society meeting in Oakland in 1991. My thanks to Patrick Mire for his help in clarifying several points regarding Charlene and the Richard community, and to the readers for their guidance and expertise, so generously shared.

1. For a fictional account of the use of *ex voto* in a local saint's cult, see Isabel Allende's short story, "A Discreet Miracle." Though the tone is humorous, the portrayal of votive practices is interesting and accurate for the culture. There are the pilgrimage to the grotto of Juana of the Lilies, pictures of the saint, medals, flowers, candles, published notices of thanksgiving in newspapers, memorial plaques, orthopedic devices, and miniature replicas of organs allegedly cured (Allende 1991). Another story in the same collection, "Clarissa," also involves a popular non-canonized saint.

References

Allende, Isabel. 1991. *The Stories of Eva Luna*, trans. Margaret Sayers Peden. New York: Macmillan.

Benedictine Monks of St. Augustine Abbey, Ramsgate. 1989. *The Book of Saints*, 6th ed. London: A & C Black.

Berger, Peter L. 1970. *A Rumor of Angels: Modern Society and the Rediscovery of the Supernatural*. New York: Doubleday Anchor Books.

Berry, Jason. 1992. *Lead Us Not Into Temptation*. New York: Doubleday.

Brown, Kimberly. 1989. Charlene Richard: What Brings Strangers to This Child's Grave 30 Years After Her Death? *Sunday Magazine* (Baton Rouge, Louisiana) 6 August: 3–8.

The Catholic Encyclopedia. 1967 edition. New York: McGraw Hill.

Chessher, Melissa. 1991. The Unbearable Lightness of Believing. *American Way* 15 May: 73–79, 104–05.

Delooz, Pierre. 1983. Toward a Sociological Study of Canonized Sainthood in the Catholic Church. In *Saints and Their Cults: Studies in Religious Sociology, Folklore and History*, ed. Stephen Wilson, 189–216. Cambridge: Cambridge University Press.

Falassi, Alessandro. 1985. Catherine of Siena: Life, Death, and Miracles. *New York Folklore* 11: 109–34.

Fish, Lydia. 1982. Ethnicity and Catholicism. *New York Folklore Quarterly* 8: 83–92.

———. 1984. Father Baker: Legends of a Saint in Buffalo. *New York Folklore* 10: 23–33.

Galanti, Elisabella. 1988. *Per Gracia Ricevuta*: Aspects of Italian *Ex Voto*. *International Folklore Review* 6: 78–85.

Griffith, James S. 1987. "El Tiradito and Juan Soldado: Two Victim Intercessors of the Western Borderlands." *International Folklore Review* 5: 75–81.

———. 1992. *Beliefs and Holy Places: A Spiritual Geography of the Pimería Alta.* Tucson: University of Arizona Press.

Gutierrez, Barbara Lenox. 1988. *Charlene.* Lafayette, Louisiana: Privately published. (Revised, updated edition of *Charlene, A Saint From Southwest Louisiana?*, Privately pub., 1979.)

Hensgens, Katie. 1990. Interview with author. Crowley, Louisiana, 18 July.

Hole, Christina. 1965. *Saints in Folklore.* New York: M. Barrows and Company.

Hollier, Earline Richard. 1989. Interview with author. Richard, Louisiana, 4 August.

Hufford, David J. 1985. Ste. Anne de Beaupré: Roman Catholic Pilgrimage and Healing. *Western Folklore* 44: 194–207.

Link, Delia. 1990. Interview with author. Richard, Louisiana, 18 July.

Low, Setha M. 1988. Medical Doctor, Popular Saint: The Syncrelic Symbolism of Ricardo Moreno Canas and José Gregorio Hernandez. *Journal of Latin American Lore* 14: 49–66.

Macklin, June. 1988. The Two Faces of Sainthood: The Pious and the Popular. *Journal of Latin American Lore* 14: 67–91.

Margolies, Luise. 1988. The Canonization of a Venezuelan Folk Saint: The Case of José Gregorio Hernandez. *Journal of Latin American Lore* 14: 93–110.

The New Catholic Encyclopedia. 1967. Washington, D.C.: Catholic University of America.

Richard, Dean. 1989. Interview with author. Richard, Louisiana, 4 August.

Richard, Mary Alice. 1989. Interview with author. Richard, Louisiana, 4 August.

Santino, Jack. 1982. Catholic Folklore and Folk Catholicism. *New York Folklore Quarterly* 8: 93–106.

Sigur, Monsignor Alexander O. 1994. Telephone interview with author. Lafayette, 6 August.

Slater, Candace. 1986. *Trail of Miracles, Stories From a Pilgrimage in Northeast Brazil*. Berkeley: University of California Press.

———. 1990. *City Steeple, City Streets: Saints Tales from Granada and a Changing Spain*. Berkeley: University of California Press.

Slazinki, Erick D. 1988. Holy Images: A Brief Study of Folk Religious Belief. *Pennsylvania Folklife* 37: 128–31.

Wilson, Stephen, ed. 1983. *Saints and Their Cults: Studies in Religious Sociology, Folklore and History*. Cambridge: Cambridge University Press.

———. 1983. Cults of Saints in the Churches of Central Paris. In *Saints and Their Cults*, ed. Stephen Wilson, 233–60. Cambridge: Cambridge University Press.

———. 1983. Introduction. In *Saints and Their Cults*, ed. Stephen Wilson, 1–53. Cambridge: Cambridge University Press.

Ôte Voir Ta Sacrée Soutane

Anti-Clerical Humor in French Louisiana

BARRY JEAN ANCELET

Though devoutly Catholic, Cajuns and Creoles have also been traditionally anti-clerical, as shown in Carl Brasseaux's study of French and Spanish colonial records,[1] which he found teeming with accounts illustrating a general resistance to the superimposition of European values among the fiercely independent colonists. Many of these sentiments developed on the frontier in New France where the *coureurs de bois* openly defied missionary efforts and even actively campaigned, as Brasseaux found, "to discredit the missionaries in the eyes of their potential Indian converts, thereby extinguishing the religious threat to their way of life."[2] Among other things, missionaries were hellbent on preventing the early colonials from engaging in sexual relations with Indian women, a very unpopular stand since European women were as rare as empty pockets on a frock. Brasseaux also notes "a remarkable lack of enthusiasm among the colonists for the church construction," a church finally built in New Orleans fully nine years after the founding of the post, long after the construction of the "numerous cabaret and billiard halls."[3] Few attended services once there were churches, prompting Father Raphael to complain, in 1725, that there was "no difference between Lent and Carnival, [between] the Easter season and the rest of the year."[4]

In colonial Louisiana, anti-clerical attitudes were also inspired, at least in part, by the dubious reputation of the

From *Louisiana Folklore Miscellany* 6 (1985): 26–33. Reprinted by permission of the author.

clergy on hand. As Brasseaux points out, "Louisiana's vicar general acknowledged, in 1725, that many priests sent to Louisiana had been interdicted in their [respective French] dioceses and fled to Louisiana to avoid punishment from their disorderly lives," vividly illustrated in the case of the illegitimate child "sired by Father St. Cosme and in Father Beaubois's attempts to seduce Governor Etienne Perier's pretty French-born *domestique* in the confessional."[5]

Frontier attitudes were later reinforced by sentiments imported from eighteenth-century France where revolutions and reforms separated church and state and gave rise to irreverent humor which survives in Louisiana French oral tradition, particularly in the treatment of the clergy as a continuation of the colonial mentality, further underscoring traditional attitudes concerning the church and its contemporary missionaries. Much in the way that the oil industry has allowed for the continuation of the frontier spirit with its adventure-laden routine, the continuing presence of missionaries in present-day Louisiana has preserved the anti-clerical attitudes they have always engendered. As late as 1970, the vast majority of parish priests in Louisiana were French, Belgian, French-Canadian or Irish missionaries. The vicar of the predominately Catholic Diocese of Lafayette complained in 1978 that the per capita rate of vocations in French Louisiana was only one-fourth that of the predominately Protestant Savannah area.

In Louisiana, stories about the church and its clergy do not take on all of religion, as they do in France and Quebec where the demise of the theocracy brought the whole system down with it. The questionable moral character of many colonial priests, along with their ill-concealed colonial mission of bringing "civilization" to an ostensibly backward people, brought about a demystification of the frock and a spirit of rebellion among the flock. This attitude is concisely expressed in an expression traditionally used to call the question during an argument, "*Ôte-voir ta sacrée soutane et je vas te montrer quelle sorte d'homme que t'es!*" (Take off that damn cassock and I'll show you what kind of man you are!) This principle is related to the infallibility of the Pope. As long as a priest speaks in church about religious matters, things go relatively

well. However, as soon as he begins to speak on social matters, he is expected to leave his cassock in church. A parish
priest who tried recently to convince a local bar owner to dis-
continue his *bourre* and poker games was told flatly, "Listen,
father, you stick to bingo and I won't say Mass."

The expression, *"Est-ce que t'as jamais vu un prêtre maigre?"* (Have
you ever seen a skinny priest?) further demonstrates the
perception among the Cajuns that members of the clergy *are*
"bons vivants" who do not always defer their gratifications to
the next life. A traditional response to the greeting, *"Comment*
ça va?" (How's it going?), is *"Mieux que ça et les prêtres seraient*
jaloux" (Any better and the priests would be jealous), alluding
to the perceived wealth and comfort of the clergy, an ongoing feeling which has considerable historical precedent going
back at least to the Jesuits' immense land and slave holdings
during the colonial period.[6]

Stories from colonial Louisiana like that of the officers
who stormed the church when relegated to the balcony by
the priest and that of the disturbance caused by Attorney
General and Mrs. Fleuriau and the wife of Superior Council
member Perry who openly berated Father Raphael when he
chided them for disturbing his sermon with their tittering
illustrate well the difficulty colonial priests had in controlling
and influencing their parishioners.[7] These kinds of stories
persist in contemporary oral tradition. Cajun delight in relating quite unsolicited accounts which reflect the survival of
colonial attitudes. The oral history of Vermilion parish includes
stories about a pastor in nineteenth-century Abbeville who
was involved in a high-noon style main street gunfight.
Descriptions of the first church service in Cankton, on the
edge of the *Marais-Bouleur* in St. Landry Parish, an area renowned
for its toughness, shows that things had changed little by the
1920s. According to these accounts, the arrival of the church
was unpopular among the area ruffians who considered such
forms of socialization a threat to their way of life, paralleling
the sentiments of the early *coureur de bois*. During the dedica-
tion of the church, several men rode into the building on
horseback, shooting out the kerosene lamps and scattering
the women in attendance, all in fine frontier style. They are

said to have been severely dealt with by an even tougher parish priest. In the wild-western tradition of pinning badges on the best gunfighters to channel their energies on the side of the law, the bishop had foreseen the difficulty of the situation and sent Père Danduron, a Quebecker who was as reputed for his physical prowess as for his religious conviction.[9]

Despite regular admonishments from parish priests, bare-knuckle duels continued to be set just after Sunday mass well into the 1950s. Gambling and cock-fighting survived the prohibitions of colonial and contemporary authorities alike and thrive to this very day.[10] Even as late as the mid-1960s, church services continued to be disrupted by the laughter of the men who preferred to stand outside the church door to smoke and tell jokes instead of going inside to hear mass. Folktales in current Louisiana French oral literature also reflect such irreverent disruptions. One example describes a nearly deaf parishioner who visits his parish priest to have an announcement made concerning a cow he has lost. He carefully explains to the priest that she should be easy to recognize since she is afflicted with a hollow horn and a spoiled teat. After his homily, the priest began his announcements with the bans of marriage. "There is the promise of marriage between Jean Broussard, son of Mr. and Mrs. Auguste Broussard, and Annette Cormier, daughter of Mr. and Mrs. Pierre Cormier. . . ." Just then, the parishioner stood up to remind the priest, "Don't forget to tell them that she has a hollow horn and one spoiled teat!"[11]

Devout and practicing Catholic storytellers often spice their sessions with a few jokes about the clergy and religious orders. Priests in jokes get little more respect than did Father Raphael in colonial New Orleans. The following story about the priest who died when his head was "turned straight" is as full of indirect disdain for the role of the priest as it is of native humor.

One day, a country priest was on his way to say mass in the next town, and he didn't have a car. He had a long way to go, so he tried to thumb a ride, but no one would pick him up. Finally, a fellow on a motorcycle stopped and offered him a ride. The priest wasn't too sure. "I don't know," he said.

"It's kind of cold to be riding on a motorcycle." The fellow said, "Well, just turn your jacket around to break the wind and you'll be okay." The priest had a long way to go, so he decided to take a chance. He turned his jacket around and they took off down the road.

A few miles later, they skidded off the road and into a ditch. By the time the police and ambulances arrived, a considerable crowd had already gathered. The authorities went down into the ditch to check the situation out "What happened?" they asked. "Well," someone answered "these two guys on this motorcycle had a bit of an accident. That fellow over there with the helmet, it looks like he's going to make it, but that one over there with the black coat, I'm not sure. His head was turned completely around. We turned it back, but I think we lost him anyway." [12]

In the title expression, "*Ôte voir ta sacrée soutane et je vas te montret quel sorte d'homme que t'es*," the cassock is rejected as an improper cover in man-to-man dealings. Here, taken at face value, it falsely defines the man and becomes the indirect cause of the priest's undoing.

Other stories directly confront the priest with irreverent retorts. One tells of a priest who told his congregation that if they prayed hard enough and gave money, they would one day see the Virgin Mary. After several years, he sensed that his congregation was getting restless, so he arranged for a young lady from a distant town to dress like the Virgin and descend on a swing through a trapdoor in the church ceiling. That Sunday, he gave the signal, saying, "Lift up your eyes and see the Virgin." As the maiden came through the trapdoor, a nail caught the bottom of her dress and lifted her dress as she descended, exposing her to the entire congregation. When the priest saw this, he said, "Lower your eyes or you will lose them." An elderly man in the back covered one eye and retorted, "Hell, at my age, I think I'll risk one." [13] Another tells of a priest and a Baptist minister debating theology while walking in the country when they see a child playing in the middle of the road. As they get closer, they notice that the child is playing in a pile of shit. The priest asks him what he is doing. The child responds that he is making a statue of a Baptist minister.

The priest asks why not a Catholic priest. The child snaps, "Because I don't have enough shit."[14] Another story has the priest admonishing his parishioners. "Don't you know that Christ died for you?" bellows the priest. From the back of church comes, "Hell, we didn't even know he was sick."[15]

Another of the problems which faced colonial priests involved their perceived lack of morals, fueled by such exploits as those of Father St. Cosme and Father Beaubois to which I alluded earlier. Indeed, many of the stories about the morality of the clergy are set in the confessional[16] and involve an unexpected reaction from the priest with which he inadvertently exposes his dubious morals, such as the one about the man who came to confession to say that he had held his fiancee's hand. The priest pointed out that this was no sin, "Is that all you did?" "No," the man replied, "I kissed her a bit." "That also is not a sin," said the priest. "Is that all you did?" "No," admitted the man, "we took all our clothes off and lay together on the bed." "Now you're getting close," said the priest. "Is that all you did?" "Yes," said the man, "that's all I did." "You're sure that's all you did?" insisted the priest. "Yes," said the man. "Well, in that case," said the priest, "for your penance, I want you to eat a bale of hay." "A bale of hay? But, Father, I'm not a horse," protested the man. "No," replied the priest, "but, if that's all you did, then you're just as stupid."[17] Another example has the priest confessing to a man who admits to having had extra-marital relations with a certain woman. The priest insists that he must reveal her identity as part of his atonement. Later, the man discovers the priest in bed with the woman. He eventually goes back to confession to admit to having stolen a dozen eggs. When the priest asks where the eggs are now, the man retorts, "Oh, no, you fooled me with the woman. I'll be damned if you'll get the eggs."[18] In addition to the obvious sexual reference, the attitude implied here, that rich priests bleed their already poor parishioners, was prevalent in colonial Louisiana and the perception persists. Built-in rituals like drinking wine out of golden chalices studded with jewels in the performance of their duties has done little to exonerate priests in the public mind over the years.

Tales about the sexual activity of priests are not restricted to the confessional setting. One example concerns a priest visiting the home of a friend to care for his wife while his friend is away on a trip. The man hides the forks under the sheets of the visitor's bed. When the man returns, the priest exposes his seduction of the man's wife when he reports that all went well except for the strange loss of all the forks in the house.[19] Another example tells of a young man who is caught in a dilemma. The mother of his girlfriend will not consent to a wedding before verifying his physical endowment. He claims embarrassment, but also fears that he will not stand up to the test. He confides his predicament to the local priest who offers to stand in for the young man. The boy explains that he is embarrassed to show his face during such a trial and arrangements are made to conceal the priest's identity. On the appointed day, the two hide in the attic. The priest exposes the part in question through a knot hole in the ceiling and the boy speaks to mother and daughter. The mother whispers her approval, but tells her daughter that she would like to share this wonderful experience with her own mother. Grandmother is ushered in and told to look up, to which she exclaims, "Well, what in the world is Father LeBlanc doing in the attic?"[20]

Sometimes, sexual activity is more subtly implied, as in the story of the two beggars who meet near the end of a road. One tells the other that it is of no use to continue to the last house because they are Catholic fanatics. The beggar continues anyway, armed with a plan. When the couple asks if he is Catholic, he exclaims, "Purebred! My father was a priest and my mother a nun."[21] Nuns are also considered fair game in oral tradition. Another story has two French nuns arrive in New Orleans to visit America. Wishing to emerge themselves in the American experience as soon as possible, they stop for a hamburger at the first opportunity, explaining their motives to the waiter who apologizes that he is fresh out of hamburgers, but can offer hot dogs instead, which are just as American. They don't know about hot dogs but finally agree. When the first nun receives her hot dog, she opens it and just as quickly closes it. After a minute, the other nun says, "You're not eating your hot dog. Is it not good?" "No," she replies, "it's not that. I just wanted to wait to see what part of the dog you got."[22] Of the two interpretations possible here, one had to do with a play on the ignorance associated with celibacy. The other implies a preoccupation with sexual connotations, even more explicit in a similar story about two nuns who go to the market to buy themselves each a banana. The vendor tells them that they are ten cents apiece but they can get three for a quarter. One nun tells the other, "Let's go ahead and get three. We can always eat the other one."[23]

Members of the clergy fare no better on the steps of the Pearly Gates. One tale, told to me by a Cajun priest, has a priest arrive at the Gates of Heaven only to be told that he must first atone for his cussing on earth by climbing a ladder and marking his sins on the way up with a piece of chalk. He starts climbing and counting. After what seemed an eternity, he heard someone above him on the same ladder asking him to move over so that he might pass on his way down. As they crossed, he recognized his former monsignor who had died earlier. He took heart that he must be nearing the top, but his hopes were dashed when the other priest explained that he was simply descending for more chalk.[24]

Folktales, legends and oral history are stylized reflections of a symbolic past. However, they often accurately reflect psychological truth. The way people feel about their past and the kinds of things they think are funny can help color the picture drawn by the facts. The abundance of the anti-clerical humor in Cajun culture would seem to debunk the pastoral image of the Acadians as the tame and devoted flock of local cure popularized by Longfellow's "Evangeline." The independence expressed in the Cajuns' anti-clerical oral literature is based on the notion that priests and nuns are unnecessary mediators in the direct relationship they enjoy with their Deity. In their own stories, the Cajuns clearly believe in God, but in their own terms and not without a keen sense of humor, as the ending of this final story indicates.

In the words of most of my informants, this really did happen to me. While driving home one evening, I noticed that one of my tires was low, so I stopped at a service station to have it fixed. There were four or five people on duty, but no one felt like working on a flat tire. They told me to come back in the morning. I knew that the leak was slow enough to last until then, but I was miffed at the lack of cooperation among the attendants. I put some air in the tire, enough to make it until morning. Then, I told the attendants that I was sorry for having inexcusable timing to stop in at such an hour, that the next time I would wait until a decent time of day to have a flat, and drove off in a huff.

After a few blocks, my passenger and long-time friend, Rick Dugas, asked if I was going to let them get away that easily. I answered that I felt like I had said what I wanted to say, but he pointed out that my cynical bullet had flown ineffectively over their heads. Now, Rick is a remarkably resourceful member of the real life community that thrives outside the walls of my university, and I've learned from experience to respect his judgment in such matters, so I asked him what he had in mind. He said, "Just leave this to me and I'll show you how to reach them."

When we arrived at my apartment, he called the station with a request for road service. He told them that he was in a green Porsche and had run out of gas in the parking lot of a Burger King restaurant across from the university campus, that he was late for a date and desperate, that price was no object. After some discussion with his hand over the receiver, the attendant said he'd come out, but that it would cost fifteen dollars plus the gas. Rick said that was fine. We then went to Burger King, got something to eat and walked across the street to watch the action from the steps of the French House. Sure enough, one of the attendants showed up after about five minutes. After ten minutes of looking for the nonexistent Porsche and talking to most of the people in the restaurant including the manager, he finally figured out that he had been had and left.

We enjoyed the show and left after he did, still chuckling about the whole scene. I noted that we had indeed gotten his goat, but Rick pointed out that he was not yet finished with his project. When we arrived back at my apartment, he called the station again and said, "Now, don't you think it would have been easier to fix that flat?" He hung up, turned to me and said, "Now they know how mad you were."

I told Rick that I thought the whole affair was a masterpiece in culturally appropriate revenge, but that we'd both burn a little in purgatory for what we'd done. After all what would Father Edwards (our local parish priest) say? He shot back, "No, man, you still don't understand. You see, God usually takes care of things like this, but He's real busy, see, and He doesn't mind if someone takes up a little of His slack."[25] I found myself faced with an indisputable example of frontier religious justice, in which priests and nuns are tolerated at best as long as they stay out of the line of fire.

Notes

1. As discussed by Carl Brasseaux in "The Immoral Majority in Colonial Louisiana," unpublished manuscript.
2. Ibid.
3. Ibid.
4. Ibid.
5. Ibid.
6. Ibid.
7. Ibid.
8. Brasseaux, interview, March, 1984.
9. From numerous oral history accounts recorded by BJA.
10. The last bare-knuckle Sunday duel I remember seeing was in 1959, behind the neighborhood grocery store. Colonial authorities made numerous unsuccessful attempts to eliminate gambling in eighteenth-century New Orleans. More recently, the Louisiana State Legislature recently went on record (reluctantly) to declare cockfighting "not illegal." Local *bourre* and poker games are left unmolested "as long as the house does not officially take a cut."
11. Told by Burke Guillory, translated from the French; field recording by BJA; AT type 1832L* *A Woman Orders a Mass to Be Said for her Stolen Ox* (for all tale type references, see Antti Aarne and Stith Thompson, *The Types of the Folk-Tale* (rev. edition, 1961), FF Communications, no. 184).
12. Told by Claude Landry, translated from the French; field recording by Barry Jean Ancelet; motif J1942 "Inappropriate medical treatment due to ignorance" (for all motif references, see Stith Thompson, *Motif-Index of Folk-Literature.* FF Communications, nos. 106–09, 116, 117, Helsinki, 1932–1936 (rev. Bloomington, 1955–1958).

13. Told by Rick Dugas; field interview by BJA; AT type 1839* *Making Thunder*.
14. Told by Burke Guillory, translated from the French; field recording by BJA; cf. AT type 1832B* *What Kind of Dung?*
15. Told by Revon Reed, translated from the French; field recording by BJA.
16. Cf. AT types 1800–1809 *Jokes Concerning the Confessional*.
17. Told by Burke Guillory, translated from the French; field recording by BJA.
18. Told by Bob Mayer; field interview by BJA.
19. Told by Adley Gaudet, translated from the French; field recording by BJA.
20. Told by Fred Tate, translated from the French; field recording by BJA.
21. Told by Lazard Daigle, translated from the French; field recording by BJA; Thompson motif J2461.2, "Instructions concerning greetings are followed literally."
22. Told by Elizabeth Landreneau, translated from the French; field recording by BJA; AT type 1339 *Fool Doesn't Know Sausage*.
23. Told by Stanislaus Faul, translated from the French; field recording by BJA.
24. Told by Father Calais; field interview by BJA; AT type 1738C* *Chalk Marks on Heaven's Stairs*.
25. Memorate.

12

The Social and Symbolic Uses of Ethnic/Regional Foodways

Cajuns and Crawfish in South Louisiana

C. Paige Gutierrez

A tourist, stepping off the plane at the New Orleans International Airport, is confronted with an array of commercial products found in no other part of the United States. Airport gift shops sell the city's heritage in the form of freeze-dried gumbo mix, plastic-wrapped pralines, voodoo paraphernalia, Dixieland jazz records, and dark-skinned "quadroon" dolls dressed in ruffled antebellum hoop skirts. Scattered among these New Orleans artifacts are souvenirs of a different kind—those that are more properly associated with Cajun country, which lies to the southwest, west, and northwest of the city. Prominent among the Cajun-oriented products is the image of the crawfish (or "crayfish" or "crawdad," to the unacculturated tourist). A visitor leaving New Orleans and venturing into Cajun country will find even more commercial crawfish iconography: plastic crawfish key chains and combs, real crawfish frozen into clear acrylic paperweights shaped like the state of Louisiana, children's books featuring anthropomorphized crawfish as main characters, and expensive gold or silver crawfish pendants. The tourist will also notice that these emblematic crawfish are frequently juxtaposed with verbal expressions of

From *Ethnic and Regional Foodways in the United States: The Performance of Group Identity*, edited by Linda Keller Brown and Kay Mussell (1984): 169–82. Copyright © 1984 by University of Tennessee Press. Reprinted by permission of University of Tennessee Press.

ethnic/regional consciousness. The words "Cajun," "Acadian," "Cajun Country," and "Louisiana" often appear in conjunction with crawfish imagery; for example, a popular local license plate and T-shirt show an upraised fist holding a crawfish, with the accompanying slogan "Cajun Power."

Even though these souvenirs are commercial products that have appeared as a response to a rise in tourism during the past two decades, they are also indicative of a strong symbolic association involving Cajuns, crawfish, and region that reaches beyond the walls of the souvenir store. The crawfish—both as animal and as food—is the predominant ethnic and regional emblem for Cajuns and for southern Louisiana.

The word "Cajun" implies both an ethnic and a regional identity. The French who settled in Nova Scotia in the seventeenth century became known as Acadians. They prospered in Canada until 1755, when the British destroyed their holdings and ousted them from Acadia. After three decades of wandering, large numbers of Acadian refugees settled permanently in southern Louisiana, where they eventually became known as "Cajuns." Cajun lifeways in Louisiana developed in response to a physical environment that included swamps, bayous, marshes, and prairies, and a social environment that commingled continental and Caribbean French peoples, Germans, Spaniards, Blacks, Indians, Anglo-Americans and others.[1] Cajuns adapted successfully to the various physical environments of the area and acculturated much of the non-Cajun population to the Cajun lifestyle. Thus, there are many people in southern Louisiana today, who, though not descended from the Acadians, call themselves Cajuns and/or participate widely in Cajun culture.[2]

Although it is impossible to define fully the word "Cajun," it has been suggested that "a Cajun is most emphatically identifiable as an individual who is typically Roman Catholic, is rural or of rural extraction, emphasizes kinship relations over those of nonkin-based associations, and who speaks or understands both English and Louisiana French languages or has close relatives who do so."[3] In addition, south Louisiana remains the homeland even for a Cajun residing elsewhere. Cajun culture has shaped and has been shaped by geographic region. Despite the incursions of the modern world (which sometimes actually strengthen regional identity, as is the case with the oil industry and its contribution to the growth of new Cajun occupations such as roustabouting and petroleum engineering), Cajun Louisiana in many ways still conforms to Zelinsky's definition of a traditional region:

> These regions are relatively self-contained, endogamous, stable, and of long duration. . . . An intimate symbiotic relationship between man and land develops over many centuries, one that creates indigenous modes of thought and action, a distinctive visible landscape, and a form of human ecology specific to the locality. Although the usual processes of random cultural mutation, the vagaries of history, and some slight intermixture of peoples, and the diffusion of innovations of all sorts prevents the achievement of total stasis or equilibrium, or complete internal uniformity, it would not be unfair to characterize such a traditional region as one based on blood and soil. In the extreme, it becomes synonymous with a particular tribe or ethnic group.[4]

The interplay of ethnicity and region, of "blood and soil," is implicitly recognized in the Louisiana state legislature's designation of a twenty-two-parish area of southern Louisiana as "Acadiana"—a term derived from the fusion of the words "Acadian" and "Louisiana."

When mainstream America came to Acadiana in the twentieth century in the form of forced English-language education, the mass media, the petrochemical industry, and World War II, the Cajuns found themselves in a position not unlike that of the newly arrived Old World immigrants to the United States. Although this "new world" of the outsider offered many opportunities for a better life, it also threatened to destroy that which was traditional and meaningful in the old life. Local customs were often ridiculed by the more "sophisticated" outsiders, and the use of the French language in advertising, legal documents, and in public schools was forbidden by state law. Many outsiders, and insiders as well, associated Cajun culture with ignorance and poverty.

However, the minority and ethnic revival movements which occurred throughout the United States in the 1960s and 1970s have parallels in southern Louisiana. The Council for the Development of French in Louisiana (CODOFIL) was founded in 1968 and has since sought to strengthen the French component or Cajun identity through language education programs, heritage festivals, publications, and cultural exchanges between Louisiana and France, Quebec, and other French-speaking parts of the world. CODOFIL and related organizations best represent the "Genteel Acadians," the wealthier or more formally educated Cajuns, who have chosen the speaking of standard French as a key rallying symbol for their ethnic revival movement.[5] These Genteel Acadians are opposed by the less organized, but equally verbal, "Proud Coonasses," who often speak a nonstandard Louisiana French dialect or no French at all, and who emphasize the playful and sometimes rowdy side of Cajun life, with its heavy drinking and eating, gambling, cock fighting, and barroom brawls.[6] A popular bumper sticker sums up the Coonass philosophy: "Happiness in Cajun Land is Gumbo, Go-Go, and Do-Do"—food, sex, and sleep. The Proud Coonasses have taken a term once used by outsiders as an ethnic slur and transformed it into a symbol of ethnic regional consciousness. The Genteel Acadians strongly oppose the use of the term Coonass (or its pictorial equivalent) as vulgar and do not identify with the lifestyle that the term represents. On the other hand, the Proud Coonasses have little interest in learning to speak standard French and sometimes see the Genteel Acadians as elitist or hypocritical.

The conflict centering around these two symbolic acts—the use of standard French and the use of the term Coonass—is reminiscent of Barth's observation that ethnic revivalism often brings with it a struggle between different segments of the group over the "selection of signals for identity and the assertion of value for these cultural diacritica, and the suppression or denial of relevance of other differentiae."[7] Although the struggle between the Genteel Acadians and the Proud Coonasses continues, neither group is likely to succeed in having its chosen "signal for identity" become *the* Cajun ethnic/regional symbol. That role has been quietly assumed by the crawfish, which is flexible enough to represent both Genteel Acadians and Proud Coonasses, and the majority of Cajuns who fit in between these two extremes. The crawfish unites Cajun to each other and to their land, while it also successfully highlights the boundaries between Cajuns and outsiders.[8]

Each year between December and May the streams, ponds, swamps, and ditches of southern Louisiana produce an abundance of crawfish. It is estimated that the Atchafalaya Basin Swamp, a half-million-acre area located in central Acadiana, produces almost 6 million kilograms of wild crawfish annually, while manmade crawfish ponds produce another 5.5 million kilograms.[9] There is no way of reliably estimating the amount of additional crawfish obtained by noncommercial, Sunday crawfishermen who scour roadside ditches and swampy areas for personal consumption. Yet elderly locals claim that the supply of crawfish has dwindled over the years and look back to a time when crawfish were so numerous that hordes of them crossing the highways created traffic hazards, and housewives in low-lying areas could scoop up a bucketful for dinner from their own backyards. Crawfish farming has helped to offset the decline in the natural supply of crawfish. Both the farms and the major natural crawfish-producing areas are restricted primarily to Cajun-dominated parishes, and almost ninety percent of the crawfish harvest is consumed in Acadiana and New Orleans.[10] Some locals joke that French Louisiana lies "behind the crawfish curtain," separated gastronomically from Anglo-American north Louisiana, where crawfish are often ignored or even scorned as food.

Not only do south Louisianians monopolize the cooking and consumption of crawfish, but they also dominate the entire industry, from trapping and processing to distribution. The Cajun is the primary heir to the cultural and technological knowledge pertinent to crawfish foodways in the United States. Thus a strong association between Cajuns and crawfish is understandable. A popularized summary of crawfish legendry, sold locally as a souvenir, states that "when a bayou baby is nine days old, his mother sticks his finger in a crawfish hole, and that makes him a Cajun."[11] A similar acknowledgment of the close association between the two is expressed in the folk song below, "*Cribisse! Cribisse!*" ("Crawfish! Crawfish!"), collected in the 1930s. (The term "Frenchmen" is commonly used in southern Louisiana to refer to Cajuns.)

> *Crawfish, crawfish, got no show, baby,*
> *Crawfish, crawfish, got no show,*
> *The Frenchman ketch 'im fer to make gumbo, baby.*
>
> *Get up in the morning you find me gone, baby,*
> *Get up in the morning you find me gone,*
> *I'm on my way to the crawfish pond, baby.*
>
> *Frenchman, Frenchman, only nine days old, baby,*
> *Frenchman, Frenchman, only nine days old,*
> *Broke his arm in a crawfish hole, baby.*
>
> *Crawfish ain't skeered of a six-mule team, baby,*
> *Crawfish ain't skeered of a six-mule team,*
> *But run from a Frenchman time he see 'im, baby.*
>
> *Look all 'round a Frenchman's bed, baby,*
> *Look all 'round a Frenchman's bed,*
> *You don' find nothin' but crawfish heads, baby.*[12]

The folk song portrays the crawfish as both a living animal with a personality and as a prepared food. In Louisiana, the crawfish exists both as part of nature, in the form of a living animal, and as part of culture, when it is transformed by cooking into food. The dual role of the crawfish-as-animal and the crawfish-as-food in Cajun life is partly responsible for the creature's success as an ethnic emblem. The crawfish can be manipulated symbolically both as animal and as food, and the meaning expressed by the image of crawfish-as-animal is different from the meaning expressed by crawfish-as-food. Thus the crawfish possesses a broad range and flexibility as an ethnic/regional emblem.

The Cajun and the crawfish-as-animal thrive together in the south Louisiana environment. This camaraderie has not gone unnoticed in Cajun popular lore, where the identities of the human and the animal are playfully allowed to blur. A local legend claims that the lobsters which accompanied the Acadian refugees in their trek from Canada to Louisiana shrunk into crawfish during the exhausting journey. These crawfish remained loyal friends to the Louisiana Cajuns, even modeling their chimneyed mud burrows after the mud chimneys on early Cajun houses.[13] Such personification of the animal is not uncommon in Louisiana lore. For example, in a joke told by local comedian Justin Wilson and also found in oral tradition, a mother crawfish, speaking in a Cajun English dialect, calms her offsprings' fears of horses and cows, but tells them to "run lak de devil" when they see a Cajun, because "he'll eat anyt'ing."[14] Sometimes the personification process is reversed, and the Cajun is pictured as taking on the characteristics of the crawfish. Several informants have remarked, after eating large quantities of crawfish, "I'll be walking backwards for a week" (referring to the animals' usual form of locomotion).

There is another aspect of the animal's behavior that makes it an especially appropriate ethnic emblem: its pugnaciousness and tenacity in seemingly hopeless situations. Crawfish with claws outstretched threaten revenge on their human captors all the way from the trap to the cooking pot. Local jokes portray a crawfish sitting on a railroad track, aggressively snapping its claws at an oncoming locomotive. Cajuns view the crawfish's feistiness with respect as well as humor. Hallowell suggests that "Cajuns have taken the animal's courage as a symbol for their own cultural revival."[15] Although it would be more precise to say that the animal's courage is only one of several factors that make it an appropriate Cajun symbol, the fighting spirit of the crawfish nevertheless certainly contributes to the effectiveness of the symbol. The intrepidity and persistence of the crawfish are paralleled in the Cajuns' own image of themselves as a people who have managed to fight and survive in the face of deportation, economic hardship, social oppression, and a sometimes hostile environment.

The modern media in Acadiana are constantly finding new applications for the crawfish-as-animal emblem. For example, an outdoor urban mural in the Cajun city of Lafayette has as its focus a giant crawfish holding an oil rig in one claw. Bicentennial note cards featured a crawfish fife-and-drum corps, and 1980 presidential campaign bumper stickers pictured crawfish waving GOP flags. At the 1980 Breaux Bridge Crawfish Festival, where crawfish iconography is carried to the limit, there were T-shirts for sale illustrated with a Cajun-style band made up of crawfish musicians, and cardboard crawfish holding Dixie beer cans in their claws advertised a favorite local beverage. A local author has recently published a series of children's books about Crawfish-Man, a part-human and part-crawfish "superhereaux" whose goal it is to "keep the peace, justice and the Cajun Way."[16] A simple Cajun fisherman under ordinary circumstances, Crawfish-Man is transformed into a powerful, claw-snapping savior of Cajuns who are in trouble. Crawfish-Man is the perfect example of the personified, pugnacious crawfish.

The physical nature of the crawfish-as-animal enhances the power of the crawfish-as-food as an ethnic marker. Like other hard-shelled crustaceans, the crawfish must be boiled or steamed alive, after which the edible parts may be extracted by a rather complicated peeling process. The meat may be eaten immediately after peeling, or it may be used as an ingredient in more complicated dishes. When boiled crawfish are served, each diner is responsible for peeling his or her own crawfish. Thus participation in a crawfish boil requires special cultural knowledge in order to eat the food as served. In addition, a diner's reaction to the sight of the rather "life-like" boiled crawfish may separate the insider from the outsider at a crawfish boil. Therefore this food event is especially efficacious in highlighting ethnic boundaries.

Crawfish boils are common spring social events in southern Louisiana. They are held at private homes or at "camps" (second homes used primarily for parties or for fishing and hunting bases) and are attended by large numbers of relatives and friends. The event requires the presence of a group of people; boiling crawfish for one or two would hardly be worth the trouble. A crawfish boil begins with the acquisition of live crawfish. In the past, the crawfish were obtained directly from the environment, thus requiring that someone in the group know how to catch crawfish. Today, however, many people simply buy live crawfish by the sack at local seafood markets.

Once the crawfish arrive at the site of the boil, the proceedings become a community project. The preparations and cooking take place out of doors; it would be very messy indeed to have a crawfish boil indoors. The job of boiling the crawfish is men's work. (Cajun men are proud of their culinary skills and often do the cooking at large-scale food events.) The men first sort the live crawfish from any dead ones that may be in the sacks. This process requires dexterity if one is to avoid being pinched by the animals' claws, and care must be taken to prevent the escape of any of the animals. The live crawfish are placed in a container of water to "clean themselves out."

Meanwhile, the guests drink beer and comment on the quality of the crawfish, and the men prepare the cooking pot. They may use a large metal container, specially designed for boiling seafood, or perhaps a large metal garbage can that serves the purpose equally well. Today, the source of heat is usually a butane burner connected to a portable butane tank. The pot rests over the fire on a heavy metal tripod. The task of setting up the pot and the butane burner requires a degree of physical strength and is potentially a dangerous job. To make this task easier, Cajuns who can afford it may have complete outdoor crawfish-boil facilities, with a moveable suspended pot, a permanent butane source, and a built-in cooler that holds a keg of beer.

After the water in the pot begins to boil, the seasoning is added. A commercial seasoning mix may be used, or the host may combine the seasonings himself. Red pepper and salt are the predominant seasonings, but other items, such as onions or lemons, may be added as well. New red potatoes or corn on the cob may also be boiled with the crawfish. The water is allowed to boil until the crawfish have been sorted and cleaned, and the seasoned water is frequently tasted, discussed, and added to. When it is agreed that the seasoning is "right," the crawfish are lowered into the pot in a large metal basket. Some people prefer to steam crawfish in a lesser amount of water with a lid, although most people boil them. The "correct" way to cook them may be a topic of considerable conversation. After about ten minutes the crawfish are tested for doneness. This, too, may be a point of slight disagreement, with each man putting in his opinion.

Meanwhile, the people who are not directly involved in the cooking process (often women) have prepared the table by covering it with newspapers and laying out drinks, bread, napkins, and perhaps trays for the discarded shells. Sometimes knives or nutcrackers are provided for cracking the claws of especially large crawfish. The crawfish are served by the men, who lift the heavy basket from the pot and pour the crawfish in a great mound down the center of the table. There are usually no clearly defined "places" at the table—people simply sit down and reach for the nearest crawfish in the pile in front of them. No attempt is made to divide the crawfish into equal amounts for each person; each diner is on his own and may eat as many crawfish as possible until the supply runs out.

Because of the large number of newcomers in Acadiana, it is not unusual for a non-Cajun co-worker or friend to be invited to a crawfish boil. An outsider attending his first crawfish boil potentially faces two problems. First, a non-Cajun may take one look at a boiled crawfish and decide that it is inedible. To a Cajun, of course, crawfish are quite edible; in fact, they are highly desired as food. But to many outsiders, the crawfish, by its very nature, is inedible or even repulsive. Today in the United States, our animal foods usually bear little resemblance to the living animal by the time they reach the kitchen or the table. A hamburger does not look or act like a cow. But crawfish must be alive when first cooked, and, being alive, the main course makes every attempt to escape or pinch the fingers of the cook (or guests). In addition, crawfish, whether alive or boiled, bear a strong resemblance to insects. Live crawfish in a container squirm and crawl over each other and make hissing and bubbling sounds, and boiled crawfish still retain their small, segmented bodies, hard shells, multiple legs, antennas, and protruding eyes. Indeed, crawfish are often called "mud bugs." Since few people in the United States eat insects, it is not uncommon for an outsider to avoid eating what he perceives to be an insect-like creature. Also, some out-siders erroneously believe that crawfish are unsanitary ani-mals, because they live in the mud at the bottom of streams and ditches. One outsider remarked, "I can't believe my eyes when I drive along the interstate and see all those people dig-ging up vermin from the scum in the drainage ditches, and taking them home to eat." Cajuns, of course, are likely to be insulted by such sentiments. A person who is too afraid or too squeamish to eat crawfish is either pitied or resented, and he is certainly not invited back to the next crawfish boil.

If a newcomer decides to eat the boiled crawfish, he faces a second problem: learning how to eat the crawfish. The locals, of course, know that the only edible portions of a crawfish are its tail meat, its fat, and, in large crawfish, the claw meat. The tail is broken from the "head" (actually the head and thorax) and the tail meat is quickly removed in one piece from the shell by a twisting and pinching process that is dif-ficult to master. The intestinal vein is separated from the meat and discarded. The fat is extracted from the open end of the head by a finger or by simply sucking the head. The meat is removed from large claws after cracking them with a knife or the teeth; however, the claws of smaller crawfish are discarded.

The speed and dexterity with which a person peels craw-fish determines the number of crawfish that a person con-sumes. Not only does a person who cannot peel crawfish end up with a very light meal, but such a person looks very silly indeed. Cajuns joke about outsiders who try to eat the head of the crawfish, or who tear up the meat in removing it from the shell, or who take a full five minutes to peel and eat a sin-gle crawfish, or who eat the intestinal vein by mistake, or who absentmindedly rub an eye with a pepper-covered fin-ger. Of course, if an outsider is a guest at a Cajun crawfish boil, the hosts will be most helpful in teaching the newcomer to eat the crawfish properly. In such a situation, the Cajun is in control and holds the situationally relevant knowledge. Those who know how to eat crawfish seem to enjoy, in a non-malicious way, the ignorance of others, and take pride in being able to teach a novice how to eat properly. Sometimes an insider will peel a number of crawfish and give the meat to the guest. This is a gesture of high regard; people do not usually take time from their own peeling and eating to peel for others, unless there is a special relationship between the two people. A mother will help her child, for example, or a husband or wife who has finished eating will help the other. A high status is attached to the person who eats a great number of crawfish, as indicated by the size of the pile of discarded shells at his place. The ability to consume many crawfish is a reflection of the person's peeling skill and robust appetite, both of which are highly regarded by Cajuns. It is said in Acadiana that a newcomer can become a local only if he can learn to eat crawfish and drink dark roast coffee.

Cajun country has gained international fame in gourmet circles, and many outsiders are eager to become acquainted with the "exotic" local foodways. Although few tourists have the opportunity to attend a local crawfish boil, numerous tourist-oriented restaurants give newcomers a gentle introduction to Cajun cooking in a thoroughly American commercial setting. In such establishments, the pepper content is kept to a minimum (relative to home cooking), and boiled crawfish may be served in relatively small quantities by waitresses who graciously explain the peeling process. Or a customer may order a crawfish dinner that includes several different dishes: gumbo or stew, etouffee with rice, patties, pie, fried crawfish tails, bisque, and the familiar American tossed green salad. In the more expensive restaurants, dishes are available that would rarely if ever grace the table of the average local: avocado stuffed with crawfish dressing, crawfish casserole made with cream sauce, crawfish Newburgh, crawfish cocktail, crawfish and lettuce salad. Non-Cajun ethnic restaurants provide crawfish pizza and Chinese-style crawfish dishes. In all these dishes, the crawfish comes in the form of peeled tail meat. As such, it closely resembles shrimp in appearance, and, of course, does not require the technical knowledge necessary to eat boiled crawfish. Thus, in the heavily advertised Cajun restaurants, where tourists and their dollars are welcome, the loosening of ethnic boundaries is reflected in the setting and the food. To the outsider, these restaurants are "different" enough to be interesting, but not so different as to be threatening or unenjoyable.

Smaller, out-of-the-way restaurants also exist in Acadiana, where the clientele is more local, French is more commonly spoken, the food is more highly seasoned, the menu is relatively limited, and the atmosphere is less plush and formal (boiled crawfish are served on newspaper or cardboard, for example). Although such restaurants welcome outsiders who happen by, only the more adventurous are apt to feel comfortable in what is obviously the "insiders'" territory.

People throughout Acadiana display pride in their local foodways. Dozens of major festivals and countless smaller fairs feature Cajun cuisine for the benefit of both tourists and locals. The town of Breaux Bridge sponsors the biennial Crawfish Festival, "the world's biggest crawfish boil," during which tons of crawfish are cooked and consumed. A historical marker in the town reads in part: "Breaux Bridge: Long recognized for its culinary artistry in the preparation of crawfish. The 1958 Louisiana Legislature officially designated Breaux Bridge 'La Capitale Mondiale de l'Ecrivisse" in honor of its centennial year." However, the more elderly residents of Breaux Bridge claim that crawfish-eating was not always something to brag about. Crawfish were "poor people's food," provided freely by the swamps and streams. A story is told in Breaux Bridge about an old crawfisherman who used to take the long way home with his catch from the Atchafalaya Swamp in order to avoid the humiliation of being seen with crawfish by the Lafayette "city folk" picnicking on the levee. Today, he still must take the long way home to avoid the city folk, who now deluge him with offers to buy his crawfish. A local woman in her eighties says, "Now the big shots eat crawfish, and the poor can't afford to. I wish I had eaten more back then; now I can't afford to buy them." An item that was once free for the taking has become an expensive food with "gourmet" overtones.

The development in Louisiana of what might be called "crawfish chic" is widely felt, even in high-level international business circles, as this recent news item illustrates:

Lafayette's fame as a garden city, a mecca for gourmet
food and a "can do" community of decision-makers in

the oil industry is well-known in Abu Dhabi, United Arab Emirates.

One of Acadiana's ambassadors of good will and international trade development is Huey Lambert, vice-president of AMASAR (American Associates of Arabia), and he provides this latest report. The Mansoori Oil Field Division held its second annual "Louisiana Crawfish Dinner Beach Party" in Abu Dhabi on May 24. It was a huge success.

Huey brought 120 pounds of crawfish for the party; next year he'll have to increase the figure to 300 pounds. Around 200 people attended, 50 from Louisiana, others from France and the Middle East. They loved the food seasoned with south Louisiana pepper sauce.

Huey met a Texan in London who offered $500 for one of the two containers of live Louisiana crawfish. The AMASAR exec turned him down.[17]

This reversal of status of the crawfish-as-food is undoubt-edly related to its effectiveness as an ethnic emblem. Today people are proud to be Cajuns and proud to eat crawfish, and the memory of past humiliations can only serve to strengthen this pride.

The new role of the crawfish as gourmet food partially explains the acceptance of the crawfish as ethnic symbol by the Genteel Acadians. Tail meat may be combined with cream, wine, mushrooms, or other relatively expensive ingredients to produce any number of refined dishes appropriate for posh occasions. Even a crawfish boil may be "dressed up"; a south Louisiana department store sells special napkins, napkin rings, place mats, trays, utensils, and glasses for formal craw-fish boils. The store also offers a complete set of crawfish-emblazoned fine Bavarian china for serving all types of crawfish dishes.

On the other hand, Cajuns today are aware of the food's past low status and of the fact that some outsiders still see the crawfish as repulsive. The Proud Coonasses draw on this awareness in their own application of the crawfish as ethnic emblem. A popular bumper sticker in south Louisiana bears a message for those people who still disdain crawfish (and Cajuns): "Coonasses make better lovers because they eat anything." A similar attitude toward criticism of Cajun food habits is reflected by T-shirts that bear the words "I suck heads." In addition, a crawfish boil may be as rowdy as the hosts and guests wish it to be. A crawfish boil can provide an occasion for heavy eating, drinking, and "partying," and as such is a perfect reflection of the self-professed Coonass lifestyle.

Today, live crawfish are available only in southern Louisiana and in a few other nearby market cities. Marketing experts realize that the sales of live crawfish in non-Cajun areas would be low, but attempts are being made to expand the market area for frozen, peeled tail meat.[18] But for now, the consumption of crawfish is limited largely to south Louisiana, where one small town poet has expressed her gratitude for the animal's presence in "Grace Before a Crawfish Meal":

> *Bless us O Lord and bless these*
> *Crawfish which we are about to enjoy.*
> *Bless those who caught them, those who prepare them*
> *And give crawfish to those who have none.*
>
> *We thank you O God for this wonderful world*
> *And for all that you have put on it.*
> *And we give You special thanks O God*
> *For having put the Cajun and the crawfish*
> *Down in the same place. Amen.*[19]

Notes

1. Nicholas Spitzer, "Cajuns and Creoles: The French Gulf Coast," *Southern Exposure* 5, nos. 2–3 (1977): 140–55.
2. Jon L. Gibson and Steven Del Sesto, "The Culture of Acadiana: An Anthropological Perspective," in *The Culture of Acadiana: Tradition and Change in South Louisiana*, ed. Jon L. Gibson and Steven Del Sesto (Lafayette: Univ. of Southwestern Louisiana, 1975), p. 3.
3. Ibid.
4. Wilbur Zelinsky, *The Cultural Geography of the United States* (Englewood Cliffs, NJ: Prentice-Hall, 1973), pp. 110–11.
5. Patricia K. Rickels, "The Folklore of the Acadians," in *The Cajuns: Essays on Their History and Culture*, ed. Glenn R. Conrad (Lafayette: Univ. of Southwestern Louisiana, 1978), p. 251.
6. According to CODOFIL research, the word "coonass" was not used in Louisiana prior to World War II. When Cajun soldiers

with their "peculiar" French dialect were stationed in France, the French locals referred to them as "*conasse*"—a word originally used for a bumbling prostitute and later for a stupid person or country bumpkin. The word was apparently brought back to the United States by Cajuns and their Texas neighbors. According to CODOFIL, the unfamiliar French term was heard as "coonass" and has since been interpreted pictorially as the rear view of a raccoon with tail upraised. The term was first used as an ethnic slur against Cajuns, but in the past two decades it has been used in a positive sense by some Cajuns themselves. It has been my observation that the word is now so commonly used by many Cajuns (despite the fact that some Cajuns abhor the term) that the word is quickly losing both its negative and positive connotations and is becoming a simple synonym for the word Cajun.

7. Frederik Barth, "Introduction," in *Ethnic Groups and Boundaries*, ed. Frederik Barth (Boston: Little, Brown, 1969), p. 35.

8. See the editorial "We Are Not Coonasses!" *Louisiane Francaise* 32 (March 1980): 5.

9. Holland C. Blades, Jr., *The Distribution of South Louisiana Crawfish*, Department of Publications Research Series No. 32 (Lafayette: Univ. of Southwestern Louisiana, 1974), p. 5.

10. Milton B. Newton, Jr., *Atlas of Louisiana* (Baton Rouge: School of Geoscience, Louisiana State Univ., 1972), p. 94.

11. Leona Martin Guirard, "Talk About Crawfish," printed souvenir (1973).

12. Irene Therese Whitfield, *Louisiana French Folk Songs* (Baton Rouge: Louisiana State Univ. Press, 1939), p. 138.

13. Guirard.

14. Howard Jacobs, "The Cajun Palate," *Acadiana Profile: A Magazine for Bi-Lingual Louisiana* 2, no. 3 (Sept./Oct. 1971): 21.

15. Christopher Hallowell, *People of the Bayou: Cajun Life in Lost America* (New York: Dutton, 1979), p. 114.

16. Tim Edler, *The Adventures of Crawfish-Man* (Baton Rouge: Little Cajun Books, 1979), and *Crawfish-Man Rescues Ron Guidry* (Baton Rouge: Little Cajun Books, 1980).

17. Bob Angers, "Anecdotes and Antidotes," *Acadiana Profile: A Magazine for Bi-Lingual Louisiana* 7, no. 4 (July/August 1979): 13.

18. James C. Carroll and Holland C. Blades, "A Quantitative Analysis of the Amounts of South Louisiana Crawfish that Move to Market through Selected Channels of Distribution," Department of Publications Research Series No. 35 (Lafayette: Univ. of Southwestern Louisiana, 1974), p. 14.

19. Leona Martin Guirard, "Grace Before a Crawfish Meal," printed souvenir (undated).

13

Is It Cajun, or Is It Creole?

MARCIA GAUDET

In south Louisiana, food and food customs are a very important part of the folklife. The procurement and preparation of
food are more than simply necessities of life; they add to the
enjoyment and celebration of that life. Though Cajun and
Creole children may not know the language of their ancestors
and may hear folk tales and Cajun or Zydeco music only at folk
festivals, they eat Cajun and Creole food in their homes. They
are also likely to grow up with an understanding of the significance of certain foods and food customs in the culture—
when certain foods are eaten, how they are eaten, how they
are prepared, etc. These traditional foodways seem to be one
of the most vital elements of folklife still retained in the Cajun
and Creole cultures, and they have become powerful symbols
of group identity.

There has been much confusion about the terms Creole
and Cajun as used in Louisiana. The term Creole was originally
used in Louisiana to designate French, Spanish, or other
European people born in the colonies.[1] When the Acadians
(Cajuns) arrived, the French Creoles in New Orleans considered themselves aristocrats. They tended to be wealthy,
educated, and urban, and they were likely to own slaves. The
Acadians were poor, usually not formally educated, and rural
settlers. Thus the Creole culture was centered in New Orleans
and the surrounding areas, and the Cajun culture developed in
southwest Louisiana. The Creoles aspired to *haute cuisine* while
the Cajuns aspired to good "home cooking" with what they

From *The Best of Lafayette* 1 (1986): 15–16. Reprinted by permission of the author.

had available. Today the distinction in Creole and Cajun cooking is not as readily apparent. To add to the confusion, the term Creole has changed in meaning. Racially, it is most often used today in Louisiana to designate people of mixed African and French ancestry. In food, it is used either to designate things that are traditional old New Orleans or Louisiana aristocratic French or, more commonly, to designate French cooking with black or "soul" influence.

Some foods, such as gumbo, are considered both Creole and Cajun. A Creole banquet menu in New Orleans in 1898 included gumbo filé, crawfish *bisque, courtbouillon,* jambalaya, pecan pralines, and *café brulot.*[2] All of these, except the *café brulot,* would also be considered Cajun foods. In fact, a Cajun woman in Breaux Bridge has been credited in one article with "creating" crawfish *bisque* in 1900.[3] Since this is two years after crawfish *bisque* appeared on a Creole menu in New Orleans, one can see the difficulty in trying to determine whether certain dishes are Cajun or Creole. There are differences, however, in how each would prepare a gumbo or other dish. In general, Cajun food in southwest Louisiana is much more peppery than Creole food in the New Orleans area. Though both are spicy, Creole food tends to be more subtle in its seasoning. In addition, Cajuns historically tended to cook the whole dish together in one pot, whereas Creole cooking tended to use separate pots in the preparation of dishes.

How can one tell the difference between a Creole and Cajun dish? Sometimes it is possible. Some things have tended to remain distinctly one or the other. Bananas Foster, Oysters Bienville, shrimp remoulade, baked pompano, and anything with a separate sauce are strongly associated with old New Orleans Creole cooking, especially in New Orleans Creole restaurants. On the other hand, three distinctly Cajun dishes in southwest Louisiana are couche-couche (a fried cornmeal mush, sometimes spelled coush-coush), *les oreilles de cochon* (a confection of thin dough that is fried and shaped to resemble a "pig's ear" and then topped with cane syrup and pecans), and maquechoux (corn and stewed tomatoes). These, in general, have not become a popular part of New Orleans

Creole cooking. They are, however, popular in French Creole cooking with a black influence, particularly in the Acadiana area. Most black people in south Louisiana with French ancestry refer to themselves as Creoles, and their cooking is Creole. However, if they live in southwest Louisiana, they are very likely to cook things like *les oreilles de cochon*, typically thought of as Cajun, yet obviously very much a part of the black Creole foodways.

Whether a certain dish is part of the Creole or Cajun heritage is often impossible to determine. The line between Cajun and Creole cuisine has become rather blurred, which is understandable after generations of living in close proximity, intermingling, and intermarrying. In fact, the two terms are now often hyphenated. However, most cooks consider themselves distinctively Cajun or Creole. Perhaps the best one can say is that if the cook is Creole, the gumbo is Creole; if the cook is Cajun, the gumbo is Cajun!

Creole and Cajun foodways continue to evolve while still maintaining the early influences and innovations that made them distinctive. They most obviously reflect the French heritage, but there are also Indian (filé), African (okra), and Spanish (pepper) influences. It is also likely that there is some German influence in Cajun and Creole foodways since many people in south Louisiana with German names think of themselves as Cajuns or Creoles.

Though there are many different ways to prepare Cajun and Creole dishes, most cooks have learned through tradition the distinctive way things "should be done" in their own area, folk group, and family. Such things as whether the water added to the gumbo should be hot or cold, whether the rice added to jambalaya should be cooked or uncooked, and whether the oil should be cold or hot when the flour is added to the roux are things about which many cooks have definite opinions. This variability is typical of traditional foodways passed on to generations orally and through performance and serves to illustrate the vital and dynamic role of foodways in Louisiana culture. Though cooks may argue about the proper color of a roux and clearly assert that their way is the "right" way, they know that there are many variations that can still produce a genuine Cajun or Creole dish. As Peter S. Feibleman wrote, "Privately, they know that everything they cook is genuine, if only because they cook it."[4]

Notes

1. Lyle Saxon, et al., *Gumbo Ya Ya* (New York: Bonanza Books, 1945), p. 139.
2. Roy Alciatore, George Reinecke, and Sidney Villere, "A Nineteenth Century Creole Menu and Its Proverbs." *Louisiana Folklore Miscellany* 2 (September 1968): 105.
3. Mario Mamalakis, "Crawfish Delicasies [sic] Originated in Breaux Bridge Sixty-Three Years Ago." *Lafayette Daily Advertiser*, April 13, 1964, p. 14, cols. 4–6.
4. Peter S. Feibleman, *American Cooking: Creole and Acadian* (New York: Time-Life Books, 1971), p. 19.

Suggestions for Further Reading on Louisiana Culture

Ancelet, Barry Jean, Jay Edwards, and Glen Pitre. *Cajun Country.* Jackson: University Press of Mississippi, 1991.

Ancelet, Barry Jean. *Cajun and Creole Folktales.* Jackson: University Press of Mississippi, 1994.

Ancelet, Barry Jean, and Elmore Morgan, Jr. *Cajun and Creole Music Makers.* Jackson: University Press of Mississippi, 1999.

Bernard, Shane K. *Swamp Pop: Cajun and Creole Rhythm and Blues.* Jackson: University Press of Mississippi, 1996.

Brasseaux, Carl A. *The Founding of New Acadia.* Louisiana State University Press, 1987.

———. *Acadian to Cajun.* Jackson: University Press of Mississippi, 1992.

Brasseaux, Carl A., Keith P. Fontenot, and Claude F. Oubre. *Creoles of Color in Bayou Country.* Jackson: University Press of Mississippi, 1996.

Cagle, Madeline Domangue. Neither Spared Nor Spoiled: The Mardi Gras Chase in Choupic, Louisiana. *Louisiana Folklore Miscellany.* 1996.

De Caro, Frank, ed. *Louisiana Sojourns: Travelers' Tales and Literary Journeys.* Baton Rouge: Louisiana State University Press, 1998.

Domínguez, Virginia R. *White by Definition: Social Classification in Creole Louisiana.* New Brunswick, N.J.: Rutgers University Press, 1986.

Dorman, James H. *The People Called Cajuns.* Lafayette: Center for Louisiana Studies, USL, 1983.

Dorman, James, ed. *Creoles of the Gulf South.* Knoxville: University of Tennessee Press, 1996.

Gaudet, Marcia. *Tales From the Levee: The Folklore of St. John the Baptist Parish.* Lafayette: Center for Louisiana Studies, USL, 1984.

Gutierrez, C. Paige. *Cajun Foodways.* Jackson: University Press of Mississippi, 1992.

Hall, Gwendolyn Midlo. *African Americans in Colonial Louisiana.* Baton Rouge: Louisiana State University Press, 1992.

Kinser, Samuel. *Carnival, American Style: Mardi Gras in New Orleans and Mobile.* Chicago: University of Chicago Press, 1990.

Lindahl, Carl, Maida Owens, and Renee C. Harvison, eds. *Swapping Stories: Folktales from Louisiana.* Jackson: University Press of Mississippi, 1997.

Lindahl, Carl, and Carolyn Ware. *Cajun Mardi Gras Masks.* Jackson: University Press of Mississippi, 1997.

Mills, Gary B. *The Forgotten People: Cane River's Creoles of Color*.
Baton Rouge: Louisiana State University Press, 1977.

Nunley, John W., and Judith Bettelheim, eds. *Caribbean Festival Arts: Each and Every Bit of Difference*. Seattle: University of Washington Press, 1988.

Olivier, Rick, and Ben Sandmel. *Zydeco!* Jackson: University Press of Mississippi, 1999.

Salaam, Kalamu ya. *"He's The Prettiest": A Tribute to Big Chief Allison "Tootie" Montana's Fifty Years of Mardi Gras Indian Suiting*. New Orleans: New Orleans Museum of Art, 1997.

Sillery, Barbara. *The Haunting of Louisiana*. Gretna: Pelican, 2001.

Smith, Michael P. *Mardi Gras Indians*. Gretna: Pelican, 1994.

Tisserand, Michael. *The Kingdom of Zydeco*. Arcade Publishing, 1998.

Notes on Contributors

Barry Jean Ancelet, Professor of French and Francophone studies at University of Louisiana at Lafayette, is a folklorist and linguist who has published widely in the areas of Creole and Cajun folklore. He is the author of several books, including *Cajun and Creole Music Makers* and *Cajun and Creole Folktales*, and co-author of *Cajun Country*.

Frank de Caro is professor emeritus at Louisiana State University in Baton Rouge. He has published widely on many topics in folklore, including Louisiana folklore. Most recently, he is the editor of *Louisiana Sojourns: Travelers' Tales and Literary Journals*.

Marcia Gaudet, Doris Meriwether and Board of Regents, Professor of English at University of Louisiana at Lafayette, is the author of *Porch Talk with Ernest Gaines* (with Carl Wooton) and *Tales from the Levee*. At present, she is completing a manuscript on narratives and traditions from the former National Hansen's Disease Center at Carville, Louisiana.

C. Paige Gutierrez is an anthropologist from Biloxi, Mississippi. She lived in Louisiana while working on her Ph.D. dissertation on Cajun foodways (University of North Carolina). She is the author of *Cajun Foodways*.

The late Tom Ireland was a graduate of Louisiana State University and an instructor at Delgado College in New Orleans. Delgado established a scholarship for early childhood education in Ireland's memory in the mid-1980s.

James C. McDonald is professor of English at University of Louisiana at Lafayette. He is the editor of *The Allyn and Bacon Sourcebook for College Writing Teachers*.

Glen Pitre is an independent filmmaker and writer who has many productions and publications to his credit. He is co-author of *Cajun Country*, and his films include *Belizaire the Cajun*.

Patricia K. Rickels is professor of English and director of the honors program at University of Louisiana at Lafayette. She has published articles on Louisiana folklore and African American literature, and she co-authored two books with the late Milton Rickels.

Barbara Sillery is an independent producer/writer who has focused on documenting the culture and heritage of her adopted state of Louisiana. Among her documentary productions are *Hidden Nation* and *New Orleans Ghost Stories*. She is the author of *The Haunting of Louisiana*.

Michael P. Smith is a freelance photographer whose works have appeared in *Newsweek* and *National Geographic*. His books include *The "Mardi Gras Indians" of New Orleans* and *Spirit World: Pattern and Expressive Folk Culture of Afro-American New Orleans*.

Michael Tisserand is a freelance writer whose articles have appeared in many publications, including the *Washington Post* and *Musician Magazine*. He is the author of *The Kingdom of Zydeco*.

Questions and Topics for Classroom Discussion and Writing Assignments

James C. McDonald

Chapter 1: "Mardi Gras and the Media: Who's Fooling Whom?" by Barry Jean Ancelet

Questions for Discussion

1. What are the reasons that Ancelet gives for inaccurate and distorted media coverage of Mardi Gras in rural southwest Louisiana? What problems are caused by journalists' ignorance of the culture? Why is it that well-informed journalists often misrepresent the rituals that they describe?

2. Ancelet implies that there is something wrong about "the outsider" viewing the Cajun Mardi Gras as "quaint," "exotic," and "picturesque." What might be objectionable about this view, especially from an "insider" point of view?

3. How do the problems that journalists and documentary film-makers have understanding and reporting what they are covering compare to the problems that students have when they are asked to research and write about topics unfamiliar to them? How are the situations of students similar to those of the journalists and film-makers that Ancelet describes? How are the situations different? What can writers and researchers do about these problems?

Topics for Writing and Research

1. Write a paper examining media coverage of Mardi Gras celebrations. Look up the coverage of Mardi Gras in newspapers, magazines, websites, and/or tourist brochures aside from the coverage cited by Ancelet. How well do Ancelet's

criticisms of media coverage of Mardi Gras in rural south-western Louisiana hold up today? Do you find differences in the media coverage based on the audience or purpose of the newspaper, magazine, website, or brochure? Do Ancelet's criticisms of media coverage apply when you examine coverage of other Mardi Gras celebrations in Louisiana?

2. Write a paper comparing your insider knowledge of a celebration or ritual that you know about firsthand with media coverage of that celebration or ritual that you find on television and the internet and/or in newspapers and magazines.

3. Compare how media like newspapers, magazines, television, the World Wide Web, and tourist brochures cover Mardi Gras in Louisiana for people unfamiliar with Louisiana culture with how folklorists cover Mardi Gras celebrations in south Louisiana, as in the first five articles in this book as well as articles in folklore books and journals. Account for the differences in the coverage considering the expertise of the writers and their audiences and purposes.

Chapter 2: "Buffalo Bill and the Mardi Gras Indians" by Michael P. Smith

Questions for Discussion
1. Why does Smith begin an article about the influence of the Buffalo Bill Wild West Show with a description of the World's Industrial and Cotton Centennial Exposition in New Orleans in 1884–85?

2. What is the myth of white supremacy and social Darwinism? How were African Americans in New Orleans able to appropriate a show like the Buffalo Bill Wild West Show, which "promoted the idea that white America was divinely commissioned" to be in charge of African Americans, Native Americans, and other people of color, to celebrate their culture and to promote multiculturalism?

3. The term "carnivalesque," which Smith highlights, is often associated with the theories of Mikhail Bakhtin, who described carnival as the purest expression of a popular culture where the voices of the oppressed co-exist with and comment on the voices of the powerful and where the usual roles and hierarchies established by society can be reversed and parodied. The term "carnivalesque" here suggests political purposes for the role reversals and masking of Mardi Gras celebrations. What political purposes do the "Mardi Gras Indian" rituals serve?

Topics for Writing and Research

1. Write an essay describing how race and ethnicity can affect the meaning and experience one takes from Mardi Gras or another ritual or celebration.

2. Many recent books and films, including several books by historian Patricia Limerick, challenge the myth of the frontier and the Old West and try to account more for the experiences of Native Americans, African Americans, Mexicans, Asians, and women in their portrayals of the American West in the nineteenth century. Some of these works, including *West of Everything*, a book by literary critic Jane Tompkins about western novels and movies with a chapter on the Buffalo Bill Historical Center in Cody, Wyoming, and the movie *Buffalo Bill and the Indians, or Sitting Bull's History Lesson*, directed by Robert Altman and starring Paul Newman, specifically examine the role of Buffalo Bill and other Wild West shows in creating popular images of the Old West. Write a research paper about the myths and realities of the Old West.

Chapter 3: "Every Man a King: Worldview, Social Tension, and Carnival in New Orleans" by Frank de Caro and Tom Ireland

Questions for Discussion

1. What do de Caro and Ireland mean when they write that "Carnival both acts as an acknowledgment of New Orleans

class and caste structure and also serves as a statement that the social tension inherent in such a structure is subject to mediation not only by local forces but also by a national ethos which is ultimately greater than the regional one"? What evidence do they provide to support this claim?

2. To what extent is the "social unity" created by Mardi Gras in New Orleans "real"? That is, to what extent does Mardi Gras help to bring different people together and to resolve their conflicts, and to what extent does Mardi Gras create the appearance and feeling of unity without really helping people to address their problems?

Topics for Writing and Research
1. Considering the articles written by Smith and by de Caro and Ireland, write an essay that discusses how Mardi Gras works to create social unity yet also provides ways for African Americans and others to protest the social structure of New Orleans.

2. Write an essay that describes a public celebration or performance that you are familiar with and explains how it creates social unity. Your essay should identify and explain the important symbols of the event that you describe.

Chapter 4: "Mardi Gras Chase" by Glen Pitre

Questions for Discussion
1. What similarities and differences do you find between the Choupique Mardi Gras and other Mardi Gras celebrations such as the "Courir de Mardi Gras"?

2. Pitre suggests that the Choupique Mardi Gras rituals may be connected to medieval flagellant processions, medieval "fête de la quémande," Roman fertility rites, and even pagan rituals of renewal and rebirth. What parts of the Mardi Gras celebration suggest these rituals? How credible do you find each connection that Pitre suggests?

Topics for Writing and Research
1. Using "Mardi Gras Chase" as a model essay, write a detailed descriptive essay of a community celebration that you have witnessed or participated in.

Chapter 5: "The New Orleans King Cake in Southwest Louisiana" by Marcia Gaudet

Questions for Discussion
1. Compose a chart that traces the King Cake tradition from its origins in the Roman Saturnalia and in Christian Epiphany celebrations to various Mardi Gras celebrations in Louisiana. What patterns of commonalities and patterns of difference does your chart reveal in different periods and in different regions?

2. Why does Gaudet raise the issue of ethnicity at the end of her article? How does the Mardi Gras King Cake tradition complicate folklorists' ideas about ethnic foodways?

3. What does the importation of New Orleans King Cakes into Cajun Mardi Gras traditions suggest about the nature and "purity" of traditions? What makes a practice a tradition?

Topics for Writing and Research
1. Write a paper describing the significance of an item of food for a celebration or holiday (for example, birthday cakes, wedding cakes, or Easter eggs). You may want to conduct research for this paper in the library and the internet or to interview other people about their celebrations in addition to relying on your own experience and observations.

2. Write a research paper discussing another cultural tradition that was borrowed and adapted from another culture, such as the accordion in Louisiana music or other Louisiana foodways like filé, okra, and spicy seasonings. Why did the borrowing take place? What changes occurred in the practice and meaning of the tradition in the new culture?

Chapter 6: "Christmas Bonfires in South Louisiana: Tradition and Innovation" by Marcia Gaudet

Questions for Discussion
1. What other occasions and celebrations involve bonfires, fireworks, or other fires? What similarities and differences do you see between the fires of these celebrations and the Christmas bonfires of south Louisiana?

2. Discuss Gaudet's questions of "traditionality": "Can the bonfires still be called traditional or folk custom? What is it that makes them traditional?"

Topics for Writing and Research
1. Write an essay comparing the effects of tourism and media coverage on the Christmas bonfire tradition to the effects of tourism and media coverage on Mardi Gras or another community celebration.

2. Write an essay about the different uses and meanings of fire in traditional celebrations.

3. Gaudet writes that "The changes in the bonfire celebration reflect, among other things, the changing attitudes toward Christmas and how it should be celebrated. For some it is no longer a private or family-centered Christmas celebration but is a secular festival to entertain 'outsiders' and attract media coverage." Conduct some research about other regions' Christmas celebrations or about the history of Christmas celebrations and write a research paper about the changing celebrations of Christmas and people's attitudes about Christmas.

Chapter 7: "The Creole Tradition" by Michael Tisserand

Questions for Discussion
1. What were the main causes for the decline in Creole music? What are the reasons for its resurgence?

2. Tisserand discusses the tradition of Creole music by telling the stories of the musicians Canray Fontenot, Bois-Sec Ardoin, and Amede Ardoin rather than making generalizations about the tradition. What do these stories reveal about Creole music? Why do you think Tisserand uses stories to explain this tradition?

Topics for Writing and Research

1. Rewrite the story of Canray Fontenot and Bois-Sec Ardoin as a script for VH1's "Behind the Music."

2. Write an essay comparing the career of Canray Fontenot or Bois-Sec Ardoin to the career of a popular musician that you know. What do the lives of these musicians suggest about the similarities and differences between their music?

Chapter 8: "Hidden Nation: The Houmas Speak" by Barbara Sillery

Questions for Discussion

1. Sillery often points out that the Houmas themselves disagree about whether they should reclaim the heritage of the Houma Indians and seek official recognition as a tribe. What are the pro and con arguments about this issue? Do you think the Houmas will be able to reclaim some of the cultural and tribal ways that they have lost? Should they even try? Why or why not?

2. To what extent an ethnic group should try to assimilate into U. S. society and to what extent it should maintain its own identity, traditions, and ways of life has always been a troubling question for minority and immigrant groups in the United States. Does assimilation, as Sillery seems to suggest, involve becoming invisible and losing one's identity? What does the experience of the Houmas suggest about whether a people should assimilate into American society, maintain or reclaim its identity, or try to find some middle ground?

Topics for Writing and Research

1. Write a persuasive essay arguing whether or not reclaiming their cultural heritage after all this time will benefit the Houma people.

2. Do some research about the federal Bureau of Indian Affairs' procedures and purposes for legally recognizing a Native American tribe. Write a research paper assessing the BIA's criteria and the possible costs and benefits of this process for a Native American tribe.

3. Sillery suggests that the history of the Houmas is similar to the history of other Native American tribes in the United States. Conduct research about another tribe or nation of Native Americans, such as the Navajos or the Iroquois, and write a paper comparing them to the Houmas.

Chapter 9: "Some Accounts of Witch Riding" by Patricia K. Rickels

Questions for Discussion

1. How might someone who does not believe in witches explain the student's experience being ridden by a witch? How might the student respond to this explanation?

2. Why did Rickels ask her student whether he had ever related his story to his priest? What is significant about the student's reply, "I never thought about mentioning it to my confessor"?

3. Why does Rickels compare her students' and informants' accounts of witch riding to Cotton Mather's writings about witch riding? Why does she carefully report the age and race of each student and informant?

4. What is significant about the skin color of the witches?

5. Rickels describes what she is doing as "collecting folklore" from her students and never calls their stories of witch riding

"superstitions," although she recognizes that many people regard a belief in witches as superstition. What does the word "superstition" mean and imply? Why are some beliefs labeled "superstitions" while others are not? What attitudes are implied by naming these stories "folklore" instead of "superstition"?

Topics for Writing and Research
1. Using the student essays in "Some Accounts of Witch Riding" as a model, write a detailed narrative of a story that reveals a belief of your culture or family. The story may be an event that you experienced or a story that others have told you. This could be part of a project, like Rickels', "to collect folklore" from the class.

2. Research the beliefs surrounding the New England witch trials, including Cotton Mather's writings about Bridget Bishop, and write a paper comparing these beliefs to those in Louisiana about witches and witch riding.

Chapter 10: "Charlene Richard: Folk Veneration among the Cajuns" by Marcia Gaudet

Questions for Discussion
1. How is the cult veneration of Charlene Richard similar to the veneration of other folk saints? How is the veneration of Charlene different from most other cult devotions? What is significant about these differences?

2. What role has the media played in the development of the cult around Charlene Richard?

3. How important is it whether Charlene Richard is canonized and officially recognized as a saint by the Roman Catholic Church?

4. How are cults around a folk saint different from cults around celebrities such as Elvis Presley or other heroes and

individuals? How are these cults similar? What functions do these cults have in their cultures?

Topics for Writing and Research

1. Research the significance of saints in the Roman Catholic Church and the church's process for canonizing saints. Write a paper discussing how Charlene Richard fits or fails to fit the Catholic Church's conception of a saint.

2. Write an essay that describes and analyzes the cultural "veneration" of another individual, such as a saint, a celebrity, or a military hero.

Chapter 11: "Ôte Voir Ta Sacrée Soutane: Anti-Clerical Humor in French Louisiana" by Barry Jean Ancelet

Questions for Discussion

1. How is it that Ancelet can write that the Cajuns and Creoles of Louisiana are "devoutly Catholic" even though they are often critical of and irreverent toward priests and nuns?

2. Why does Ancelet attribute anti-clerical humor to the frontier spirit of Louisiana?

3. What is the purpose of Ancelet's concluding funny story, considering that the story does not involve religious clergy?

Topics for Writing and Research

1. Write an essay defining the "frontier spirit." Consider how the frontier spirit has changed in recent times.

2. Collect several jokes on a single topic and write an essay analyzing what the jokes reveal about the attitudes and tensions surrounding that subject.

Chapter 12: "The Social and Symbolic Uses of Ethnic/Regional Foodways: Cajuns and Crawfish in South Louisiana" by C. Paige Gutierrez

Questions for Discussion

1. Why has the crawfish been a more successful symbol for Acadiana than other symbols? What Cajun character traits does the crawfish represent? How has the popularity of eating crawfish mirrored the changes in ethnic pride and status for Cajuns?

2. How does the crawfish boil serve to strengthen community, distinguish individuals in the community, and deal with outsiders to the community?

3. In what ways has the rise in importance of the crawfish for Cajuns unified Cajuns of different social class, and in what ways has it emphasized and even exacerbated class differences?

Topics for Writing and Research

1. Write an essay that analyzes the meanings and connotations of the crawfish as a symbol on a t-shirt, a tourist souvenir, a children's book, a promotional website or brochure, or on another artifact.

2. Write an essay analyzing another symbol, like the crawfish, that is used to represent a region or an ethnic group (for example, the leprechaun).

Chapter 13: "Is It Cajun, or Is It Creole?" by Marcia Gaudet

Questions for Discussion

1. "Creole and Cajun foodways," Gaudet writes, "continue to evolve while still maintaining the early influences and innovations that made them distinctive." What are these influences and innovations? How have the two foodways evolved?

2. Gaudet writes that the traditional foodways of Cajun and Creole culture "have become powerful symbols of group identity," yet she shows that it is often "impossible" to tell the difference between a Creole and a Cajun dish. How can it be so difficult to distinguish between Cajun and Creole dishes if the foodways are powerful symbols of the identities of the Cajuns and Creoles?

Topics for Writing and Research

1. Gaudet writes that Cajuns are "likely to grow up with an understanding of the significance of certain food and food customs in the culture—when certain foods are eaten, how they are eaten, how they are prepared, etc." Choose a food that has significance for your family or culture and write an essay that describes when and how it is eaten and prepared and discusses its significance.

2. Write an essay that compares and contrasts Cajun and Creole cultures, considering foodways, celebrations, and other traditions.

Index